Helter Skelter

Diary of an Autistic Adventurer

Nicholas Robinson

chipmunkapublishing
the mental health publisher

Nicholas Robinson

Published by
Chipmunkapublishing
United Kingdom

http://www.chipmunkapublishing.com

Copyright © 2014 Nicholas Robinson

ISBN   978-1-78382-130-3

Chipmunkapublishing gratefully acknowledge the support of Arts Council England.

Prologue

2:30am, Dock 9, Salford Quays, Manchester
24th August 2013

I got into the water and adjusted my swim goggles and waited to take my turn to swim my part of the 32km relay swim that six of us where doing from Liverpool open Water swimming Club. Our swim Team was called Lorna Loonies because one of our swimmers was recovering from an Operation that she had in a Hospital in Birmingham. The water was right temperature to swim and I swum my 2km swim in 42 minutes around Dock 9, Salford Quays. Once I finished my swim another swimmer took over to do there 2km swim for the relay Swim. I got out of the water and I was very hyperactive and when I got to the changing room tent I realised that my Towel was wet as it had been raining while I was doing my 1st of 3 swims that I had to do for my part of the swimming relay team. My next swim was set for about 5:30am in the Morning.

5:30am, Dock 9, Salford Quays, Manchester
24th August 2013

I started my second swim as part of the 32km relay swim at Salford Quays dock. As I started swimming I noticed that the Sun was coming up through my swim goggles. I had a beautiful second swim with the sun rising as I swam around the course that had been laid out at the start of the Relay Swim. The Relay swim started at midnight and I was very hyperactive all the way through this event and our swimming Club swum the Relay swim at Salford quays in 11 hours and 12 minutes.

I was still very hyperactive after the relay swim had finished and when I got home it took me a while to get to sleep. I eventually went to Bed and had a really good sleep. When I got up after slept for 8 hours I made my way to the Bathroom and I look at myself in Bathroom cabinet. I smiled at myself in the bathroom cabinet mirror and once again found my fun and bubbly natured Character.

27th August 2013

I sat outside by the New Pond that Dad had made. The pond had a waterfall and a fibreglass waterwheel spinning the water round. Next to the Pond Mum had her Bird feeder and loves feeding all the small Birds. There are two ponds in the Back Garden and in the bottom garden pond we have over 30 baby fish in which I feed them. At the start of the back Garden Dad has a workshop and is usually found in his workshop making things or mending and repairing things.

I sat in the back Garden next to the new Pond and reflected how my Day had been. I was still tired from doing a 36km relay swim at Salford Quays, with five of my Friends. It had been a quiet day in work today and I enjoy listening to my Music through my headphones. Later in the afternoon I went to the Doctor's for a Medicine review and as I waited in the Doctor's waiting area, I looked at a magazine that had an article about Harrogate Turkish Spa. I really enjoy Spa days and what a lovely Adventure it would be to visit the Turkish Spa in Harrogate. Soon it was time for me to talk to the Doctor about my Medicine Review

28th August 2013

I looked at myself in the Mirror this morning and I saw my reflection in the mirror, I had put on weight since taking my over-dose in March 2013. The weight gain was due to the medicine I am on. I don't really like looking at myself in the mirror and since I have put on weight I always think I look sad when I look in the Mirror. I decided to have a Wet shave in the bathroom, I enjoy having a shave and I use a Wilkinson Sword Hydro 5 Razor. I start my wet shave using a facial Scrub by the Real Shaving Company. I make sure I wash my whole face with the Facial wash. After I have done my facial wash I shave with Real Shaving Company Shaving Gel. I have sensitive skin, to finish I use the Real Shaving Company Aftershave Balm cream. I enjoy having a wet shave and I am always happy after having a shave and I always feel good about myself. After putting on the aftershave balm I then brushed my teeth with my favourite toothbrush which is a Colgate 360. I like this toothbrush as it has a tongue cleaner which I think is a lot of fun. I took one last look in the Mirror and set of for work.

28th August 2013

When I got home I sat on a Royal Enfield GT Contental Sport Motorbike in Red. Dad had been repairing the bike for a friend and I got the chance to sit on this Classic Motorcycle. After sitting on the Royal Enfield I then made myself a filtered Coffee and sat down outside and Drunk Coffee. I sat outside and thought about the 6 mile swim I was going to on the 14th September 2013. The swim will start on the Duke of Westminster Estate at Alford Iron Bridge and then I will swim 6 miles down the River Dee to Chester Suspension Bridge. Later on in the Day I did some research on my laptop for Adventures that I have thought of doing. I looked on Amazon an online Shop as I am looking for the Book of Magic a Game for the Sony PlayStation 3. Later in the evening I became depressed as I sat in my room and looked out of my window at the street. Opposite my Bedroom there is a lamppost in the corner of the Avenue that emits a strange orange glow that I watch and sometimes it flickers on and off. I then went to bed and cuddled up with my Cuddly Toy dinosaur called Herbert. Herbert is about 2 feet long and has large teeth. I love Herbert the Dinosaur.

29th August 2013

I got home for 3:30pm and then I had a Shower using Original Source Shower Gel which I enjoy using. After I had my Shower I set the table for Tea outside. I enjoyed having my Tea outside although it wasn't as warm as I thought it was going to be and I had to put a hoodie on, which is an Animal Freesport Orange Hoody. After having Tea I went online and got a ticket for the Creep Show for the 24th October 2013 at the Perch Rock, New Brighton. The Creep Show is a scare attraction and the tour is about an Hour long. After going online I went to my bedroom and put my Wizard cloak on which is Gold and Black with crested emblem on left breast. I have lots of Wizard accessories, Wizard Wand, Wax Seal and also a Wizard scarf. At 10pm I took my medicine and made my way to bed. I enjoy eating Starbursts in bed and my favourite Ale is Wychwood Goliath Ruby Ale brewed by Wychwood Brewery. I had a text from one of my friends asking if I was going swimming on Sunday Morning. I sent a text back and said" I am excited about swimming around the Dock on Sunday".

Nicholas Robinson Hygiene

Nicholas has Asperger Syndrome and loves creating list and also likes certain products and stick to his routine. Nicholas bathing products and hygiene Products are used in a routine manner. Nicholas uses the same products as he enjoys the names and labels and the shape of the Packaging.

Nicholas Hygiene Products
Wilkinson Sword Hydro 5 Razor
Real Shaving Company, Preshave facial wash
Real Shaving Company, Shaving Gel
Real Shaving Company, Aftershave Balm
Philip Philishave wet/dry Electric razor
Colgate Toothpaste
Colgate 360 Toothbrush with tongue cleaner
Original Source Shower Gel and Shampoo

Nicholas enjoys showering with Original Source shower Gel and uses Original Source shower gel after open water swimming. Nicholas also likes the Soap Shop Lush and loves looking at all the different soaps that are on offer. Nicholas loves the friendliness of the staff at Lush and there warm smiles and knowledge of the Shops products.

30th August 2013

In my Diary I have decided to be as honest as I can. I am very bubbly character and enjoy the thrill of Adventures. I washed my Car this afternoon at 4pm with a soapy wax Shampoo, I enjoyed washing my car and see it sparkle in the Sun. after washing my Car I decided to look at my emails and I saw an event that hopefully I will be attending next Friday evening. The event I will hopefully attend will be going back to school with a strict School mistress inn charge. The event is what known as BDSM or a Radical desires evening where I will be involved in role play dressed as a naughty school girl that is Black and Red with white spots. I am looking to be very naughty in the classroom so the school mistress will give the cane across my bum and I hope it will hurt. Later in the evening I decided to have a bath and I love playing in the bath. I enjoy using different Lush Soaps and enjoy Lush Bath bombs where you put in the Bath and they fizzle away. After I had a bath I put my dressing Gown on and poured myself a Wychwood pint of Ruby Ale and then I snuggled up on my Bed with my cushions Mum had made for me. I put the television on and watched the Afro Samurai DVD; Afro Samurai is Japanese Manga Cartoon.

Nicholas Robinson Technology

Nicholas loves Technology and loves touch screen computers and loves his smartphone. Nicholas enjoys listening to Music through his headphones.
Here is the list of Nicholas Technology
Acer Timeline X Laptop, 6 GB Ram, 750 GB Hardrive
Apple IPod Classic 30GB Hardrive
Apple IPad 2, 32 GB IOS Touchscreen
2 X Skull candy Headphones, Low-rider
2 X Motorola S9-HD Bluetooth Headphones
Sony PlayStation 3 120 GB hardrive & Sony Vita 16GB hardrive.
Hitachi 26inch LCD/DVD hd Television
Sony Ericsson W395 Walkman Phone
Samsung Galaxy S2, Smartphone, 32 GB hardrive
Panasonic Bluetooth Speaker and IPod dock
Damson Bluetooth Resonating Speaker

Nicholas would like the new game console by Sony, which is the Sony PlayStation 4 and Nicholas would also like an Apple IPod touch 6th Generation with 32 GB Hardrive. Nicholas loves playing computer Games and enjoys Action/Adventure games as well as Horror Survival Games. Nicholas loves the graphics that the Sony PlayStation 3 produces and he enjoys using his Apple IPad with touchscreen Technology.

The Spiral Staircase

I have now completed my Book about my Adventures that I had done from February 2010 to May 2013. I done over hundred different Adventures and experienced lots of different things. At the end of the three Year Adventure I was to take an Overdose of my Medicine and become an Angel.

I took the Overdose in March 2013 I thought I had taken enough tablets for the overdose to work and become an Angel. I had to spend the Night on a medical Ward at the Wirral University Hospital on the Wirral. While on the Ward I prepared myself to die, I never saw anything wrong with what I did." I was ending my Book with the Character." As I write this 4 month Diary I still feel the same way, I still don't understand where I went wrong. 5 months has now

passed since I took my overdose that put me in Hospital. There is not a day that goes by that I don't think of becoming an Angel.
I try and put on a smile on my face for everyone I meet, but I am really sad that I haven't become an Angel and now I am writing my 4 Month Diary from 27th August 2013 to 1st January 2014.

The Garden of Aurora

Everyone likes a Puzzle and the Garden of Aurora is indeed a Beautiful Puzzle. The Garden of Aurora as Nicholas Describes it as his Sanctuary when he became ill. The Garden of Aurora website is a masterpiece of Psychology. The Garden of Aurora starts with two images in the Drawing. The first image of Nicholas you see is Nicholas in the Intensive Care Unit in a hospital bed. The second image you see is Nicholas on the floor with a question mark say Nicholas Adventures? The Garden of Aurora takes you on a journey from Nicholas being in Intensive care and being in the Garden of Aurora and then healing himself in the Great Spa of Aurora. The Great Clock granted Nicholas his wish to go to the Garden of Aurora and the Great Spa of Aurora. The Garden of Aurora is a beautiful piece of Art, there over 50 drawings on the website as well description of Nicholas journey through Aurora. The Garden of Aurora is one of the 21st Century greatest Psychological puzzles, the secret of unlocking the Puzzle lay in the drawing themselves, study the Drawing and enter the Garden of Aurora.

31st August 2013

I was quite excited today, I had ordered myself the Artic white Batman with the Batboat and Mr Freeze and you have to rescue Mermaid Man. I love Lego Batman and have got the Lego Batwing and the Joker with his Helicopter to make. At teatime Mum had cooked Pork chops and we had a mix grill with potatoe waffles. Later in the evening I looked on the internet at the Sandcastle Waterpark and looked at the two new waterslides they have recently built. At 10pm I had my medicine and then I had a Pint of Wychwood Ruby Ale and watched a Movie called Avengers Assemble which is Marvel Comic Book Film. With my Wychwood Ruby Ale and a big bag of Kettle Salt & Vinegar crisps. I watched the Movie for hour and a half and then I fell asleep. I woke up the next morning at about 8am. I had a coffee and a slice of toast and then after I had breakfast I got my swim bag ready for my first swim of September 2013. Autumn had arrived and my September

Adventures had come upon on me. I made sure I had everything in my swim bag to go Open water swimming this morning.

1st September 2013

I got to Queen Dock, Liverpool at 9:30am and my swim friends were waiting for me. We got changed and got ourselves ready to swim. I entered the water at Queen Dock via the slipway and the water was still a nice temperature, I swam 4 laps of Queen Dock which 2,200 metres. The wind was across the Dock this morning and making the water quite choppy. I enjoyed my swim this morning and I had a nice hot shower in the Water Sport centre.

After the swim this morning, myself and the other swimmers who did the relay swim on the 24th August 2013 at Salford Quays went to Visit a swimmer who has just had a Bone Tumour removed, I think the Lady we went to see was very brave. The day finished with three of us going for a swim at Eccleston Ferry near Chester. We had a really good swim this evening swimming up the River Dee about 1km past Eccleston Ferry and then swam back with the current. Then after we got changed we sat by the River bank and drunk Coffee and took in the Beautiful scenery the River Dee had to offer. We talked about swims we would like to do in the Future, I would like to swim Lake Zurich.

2nd September 2013

I made my way through the Liverpool city traffic and eventually arrived at Queen Dock for evening Swim. It was a great evening and the Sun was out. I got changed into my swim shorts and put my swim cap and goggles on. I use Vaseline under my arms to stop Abrasions, the skin rubbing against itself. I made my way to the slipway into the water and felt the Sun beam down on my Back and I felt the Warmth of the Sun Rays. I entered the Water and then I adjusted my goggles for the Swim in front of me. I started swimming at a good pace and I did 7 laps of the Dock tonight which is 3,800 metres. At the end of the swim I looked on the side of the Dock wall at the Marine life. I saw little fish and jellyfish and I also saw a Conger Eel that are native to Liverpool Docks. The Dock walls are very beautiful to look and there is lots of seaweed and mussels attached to the Dock wall. Before I got out I had a swim underwater and swam to the Bottom of the Dock which is very Muddy and Murky.

3rd September 2013

I arrived Home after I finished Work to find Dad in the Living Room with Water coming through the Ceiling. Dad has been putting new radiators into the House and this afternoon he tested the Pipe work system with a hose and there was a leak from one of the radiators in one of the Bedrooms.

I have been very depressed today and also paranoid, I have very depressed since I was very hyper-active at the Relay Swim in Manchester in August. I have booked myself to do an Art Course at Birkenhead Sixth Form College where I will learn to Paint with Acrylics. I hope I can create a beautiful painting and my first painting on the course I was hoping to paint the Pink Palace in Jaipur, India. I think it would make a Great Painting. As the night went dark I watched all the lights come on in the Garden and watched the four crystal Balls glow next to the new Pond Mum and Dad have built. I sat outside and enjoyed a nice autumn evening. In the Pond you could hear the Frogs croaking and jumping into the Water.

4th September 2013

I am in a lot of pain today and my head hurts and feels as if my skull is expanding and my head is starting to hurt all the time. I got home for 4pm and made my Dad a Coffee. We had Tea which was Fishfingers and Chips. I like having Heinz Tomatoe ketchup and sweet pickles when I have fishfingers and Chips with a glass of Lemonade. After the meal we had a crunchie chocolate ice ice cream. Mum and Lee have gone to the Caravan in Llanberis, North Wales for a week holiday and Dad was looking after me this week. Dad had found the leak from upstairs central heating pipes and it was my Bedroom Radiator that needed tightening up. In the evening I sent an email to Manchester University Sleep Department and I asked if I could volunteer for a Sleep study. I also registered with a depression clinical trial with a Medical Company in Salford Quays. I am looking forward to hearing from them. I like the idea of being wired up to all kind of machines and someone looking at my REM Sleep Pattern on a visual display monitor.

5th September 2013

It was a hectic day in work today, I am an Archive Clerk and work for the National Health Service. I finished work at 3pm and got home for 4pm. I had 2 parcels for me to open. The first Parcel was an Ink Cartridge for Cross mason Pen that I like writing with. The second parcel was my Lego Batboat that I ordered from Amazon online Shop. I love writing with a Cross Pen, I use a metallic Blue Cross mason Pen, the weight of the Pen is very well balanced. Also there was a third parcel that I didn't see at first, I opened the third parcel and it was a pair of Oakley Sunglasses that I have ordered and when I looked in the Mirror with my New sunglasses I thought I looked really Cool!.

The only thing was I couldn't see very well as I had to take my glasses off to put the Sunglasses on. I have always thought of the idea of getting contact lenses. I need to go to the opticians and find out if I could get a special pair of contact lenses made as I have rugby shaped eyeballs and I would love to see myself without glasses. After looking at myself in the mirror with new sunglasses I then went to my Bedroom and listened to some Music.

6th September 2013

I arrived at the BDSM club on Merseyside at 9:30pm. I got changed in the changing room and put my female mouse costume on with matching red and white headband bow. I put my naughty girl wig on and then I made my way to the Bar area of the club. I had come to the BDSM club for a school evening. The head mistress started school at 10pm and I was told off for not having a school uniform. I joined my class mates and we were very naughty and we didn't do what the head mistress told us. I had been a very naughty Girl in the class tonight.

After the head mistress took her lesson in the music room of the club. It was then time for me to receive the cane from one of the head mistresses teachers. I received the cane from one of the female mistresses on the second floor of the club. This was my first time in getting the cane, and I can say it did hurt slightly but it was pleasurable at the same time. After getting the cane I went to the Bar area and got myself a filtered Coffee and then I relaxed in one of the couches in the Lounge area. I still haven't used the Jacuzzi or wet area of the club as there is much more to the club to explore and I am starting to enjoy BDSM fetish.

7th September 2013

Dad took me to Steve Webb model Shop in Frodsham this morning. I was very impressed at the Model Shop. I looked at the Remote Control Cars and I bought myself a Losi Micro-T 1/36 scale remote control car. I am looking forward to playing with my new little remote control car. After we went to the Model Shop, we set off to Llanberis, North Wales. Mum and Lee where waiting for us at the Caravan and we had a good drive along the coastal road. On the Journey to the caravan we stopped at a roadside cafe and we had a Bacon toastie each and 2 cups of coffee. We arrived at the Caravan at 12:30pm and then I decided once we got to the Caravan to go for a swim in the river as the River runs behind the caravan park. I put my swimming trunks on and made my way down to the River. The River was running very fast and had lots of rapids and I found a gap in the river to go for a Bath. The water was very cold and the water had come straight off the Mountains. After my swim Mum had made Fish and Chips for me and Lee, for desert I had a chocolate éclair and a cup of coffee.

8th September 2013

I got up this morning and my knees hurt, my knees have been hurting me for the last three months are getting worse and I was in a lot of pain with my knee's this Morning. I spent the morning tidying up my bedroom and dusting my ornaments. It took me an hour to tidy my Bedroom and clean all the Shelves. In the afternoon I wrote some ideas that I have for a Book. I like to write on the Dining Room table next to the patio Windows where I can see the new Pond and waterfall that Dad has made. Mum and Dad had gone to their Caravan in Llanberis, North Wales for a week holiday and Lee was looking after me. At 5pm Lee cooked a mixed grill for us and I washed the dishes afterwards. In the evening I did a drawing of me going back to the Great Spa of Aurora, the Spa of Aurora is a sanctuary where I go to in my mind and is a place for me to relax and unwind.

9th September 2013

I was at work and I received a voice mail from my work Counsellor telling me that I had missed an Appointment that was at 9:15am at the Stein Centre, Birkenhead. The work Counsellor rung me again at mid-morning just to see how things where and to make sure I was alright. I told my counsellor that I was doing a six mile swim on

14th September 2013 and then the following day I would be doing a Catapult reverse bungee jump, I got really excited about telling my work counsellor all about upcoming Adventures. I finished talking with my counsellor and then I put my Skullcandy Headphones on and filed paperwork away in folders while listening to my music through my headphones. I like all types of music, but I couldn't tell anyone who is in the charts at the moment. I love listening to Led Zeppelin and Rock n' Roll Music. I listen to music as it helps me concentrate at work doing my archiving and I general listen to classical music and the music of Sarah Brightman and my favourite Song from Sarah Brightman is Nella Fantasia written and composed by Ennio Morricone from the Film the Mission.

10th September 2013

I stood in front of the Bathroom cabinet Mirror and put my anti-biotic cream on my Lip that was stitched up in Hospital after I accidently cut my lip. The anti-biotic cream I think is taking the swelling down on my lip and it looks a lot better than it did a month ago. I had seven stitches put in my Lip and the stitches have dissolved since then. After I put my cream on my lip I went down stairs to the dining room and me and Lee had Tea which was Fishfingers and Chips and I had sweet pickled onions and Heinz ketchup. In the evening I put all my Hotwheel cars on a board on the Dining Room table and put the Hotwheel cars into rows of 30, I keep my Hotwheel Cars in a Cadbury's roses Christmas tin. My favourite Hotwheel Cars are the American 1970's era, and I like the Shelby Viper Car and Ford GT500. I love Cars and I love buying a Hotwheel toy Car once a week. They sell Hotwheel cars at my local Supermarket, I like choosing from the Blue Hotwheel Container on the shelf on the Supermarket.

11th September 2013

It was raining when I finished work today and I decided before I drove home to visit the Toy Shop at Sealand Retail Park to look at the Lego Batmobile set. When I got to the Toy Store I found out that they didn't have the Lego Batmobile set in stock and I would try again another time. This evening I booked two tickets for me and Mum to go and see the Circus of Horrors on the 5th November 2013 which will be a Tuesday evening full of fright and thrills. I have seen the circus of Horror show 2 years ago in January 2011 and I thought the show was amazing. I wonder what was in store for this coming show in November. One of my swimming friends is coming with me to Farmaggedon one of the best Scare Attractions in the Country and just happens to be 10 miles away from where I live. I have also been to Farmaggedon before and I was absolutely terrified and this scare attraction has not got an 18' year's old certificate, like you see on a Movie at the cinema. The Scare Attraction that is Farmaggedon is Adult only. I hope the scarecrow is there this year as I like to get my Photograph taken with him as I like having Fun.

Condiments Nicholas Robinson Uses

Heinz Tomatoe Ketchup
HP Brown Sauce
Sweet Pickles

Favourite Meal

Fishfingers and Chips with Sweet Pickles & Tomatoe Ketchup

Crisps and Nuts

Golden Wonders Salt and Vinegar/Prawn Cocktail
KP Dry roasted Nuts
Pork Scratching.

Sweets
Maynard's Sport Mixture
Lions Midget Gems
Rowntree Fruit Gums
Rowntree Starbursts

Alcohol Drinks

Wychwood Hobgoblin Ruby Ale
Wychwood Goliath Ruby Ale
Mann Brown Bitter

Chocolate

Cadbury's Dairy Milk
Cadbury's Nut Clusters

12th September 2013

I took my Sponsorship form into work with me and everyone sponsored me for my 6 mile swim on Saturday the 14th September. I was really made up that people have sponsored me as I am raising money for the Neo-natal unit which is the Babygrow appeal. When I got home I made some filtered Coffee for myself and then Lee brought Tea in at 5pm from the Chip Shop.

I had battered sausages and Chips for Tea with HP Brown Sauce. I made sure all the animals where fed and also fed the Baby-fish in the bottom pond. In the evening I did some drawings of the Garden of Aurora and the Spa of Aurora. At 10pm I had my medicine and then I got into Bed and ate a Bag of crisps, which where Steak Grill Crunchy crisps. I watched a movie which was Alien vs Predator and they thought each other in an underground pyramid. I like watching Science Fiction films and love James Cameron Aliens film. I would love to go around an Alien scare attraction I think it would be an amazing experience. I think there used to be an Alien Scare Attraction in Glasgow but I don't think it still running now and now shut down.

13th September 2013

I had a quiet Day in work today and I enjoyed listening to my music while filing the paperwork into the folders. I was getting excited today as I am swimming 6 miles tomorrow in the River Dee. This evening I got my swim bag ready for the swim tomorrow. I washed my prescription swim goggles in washing up liquid and made sure I washed all the soap of the goggles. I made sure I had my swimming trunks and my favourite swim cap I like wearing, and made sure I Vaseline that I use under my arms to abrasions whilst I am swimming. I also made sure I had enough energy drinks for the swim as it would be a 3 hour swim and might need some sugar to keep my energy levels up. Once I got my swim bag ready I then charged up my Apple IPad 2 as I have a Music programme called Planetary which makes the Music into a Solar System, and the albums is a Sun and the tracks become planets and you can zoom in and look at the Solar System, it is a beautiful application.

14th September 2013

I got to Alford for 9am; Alford is a quite village six miles outside of Chester and was the starting point for the Bridge to Bridge swim that would be starting at 10am. I met my canoeist at the Boat house next to Alford Iron Bridge; the Iron Bridge was blue and white and looked very beautiful.

At 10am I got in to the River Dee and found it the water very cold at first. The start whistle went for the swim start and I was glad of this as I could warm myself up my swimming. I swam at a good pace and soon found myself 3 miles down River at Eccleston ferry. The second half of the swim was quite tough as the River Dee widened and there was less flow of the Current. The last mile felt as if it went on for ages. Eventually I saw the Suspension Bridge of Chester City through my swim goggles. I finish the 6 mile River Dee swim in 3 hours 5 minutes and raised £150.00 for neo-natal unit in Countess of Chester Hospital. The Day ended with me sitting outside at 10pm at Night looking at the Stars in the night Sky. I enjoyed looking at the night sky and I always thin life is out there spare on a faraway distance somewhere.

15th September 2013

Me and Dad went to Birkenhead North train station Car park to play with Dad's radio controlled motorbikes. It was a lot of fun and we played with the remote control motorbikes for a good hour. After playing with the r/c motorbikes, we then went home and Mum made everyone a cup of tea and I had a nice Nescafé Coffee. I finished the new drawing for the Garden Aurora Great Spa this afternoon. The drawing has very bright colours in it. Later in the afternoon I went too Liscard and went to Home and Bargain which is like a general store that sells just about everything you can think of. I decided to get myself some Prawn cocktail golden wonder crisps and Maynard's sport mixture sweets and Galaxy chocolate. For tea Mum cooked a mix grill and desert was cake and coffee. In the evening I started a new drawing for the Great Spa of Aurora. While I was doing my drawing I listened to some music on my Laptop. At 9pm I had a wet shave using Real Shaving Company shaving and a Wilkinson Sword hydro 5 razor. After having a wet shave I then had a shower using Original Source shower gel with Zingy Lemon. After my shower I had a Glass of cold Pepsi in a Glass.

16th September 2013

I found myself being sick in the toilet bowl in the Bathroom at 4am in the Morning I was being sick in the bathroom nearly half the night. I eventually got back to bed about 5:30am and then the alarm woke me up at 7:30am. I got out of Bed and dressed myself as best as I could then I made my way down the stairs to the Living Room. When I walked through the Lounge I saw my Dad sitting in his Chair cuddling Jessica the Cat. Dad saw that I looked unwell and told me to go back to Bed and Mum would ring work for me to tell them that I had been sick during the Night. I went back to bed and woke up at 12 o Clock midday. When I woke up I noticed that my knee's where very sore and I couldn't move my legs properly. When I got downstairs Mum made me 2 pieces of Dry toast and a nice cup of Tea. During the afternoon I did my writing of my diary and did another drawing for the Return to the Great Spa of Aurora. I also drunk lots of orange juice this afternoon and I am enjoying drawing and writing about my return to the Great Spa of Aurora. In the evening I played on my Sony PlayStation 3 and I am very excited about the launch of the Sony PlayStation 4 and the new games that are coming out.

17th September 2013

It was quite busy in work today and I had a lot of filing to put away. I had my dinner at midday and have a couple of Galaxy chocolate pieces as well for my Dinner. In the afternoon I did more filing and listened to my music using Skullcandy headphones. I also thought about how cold my obstacle race is going to be in January 2014. The obstacle course race I have entered is called tough guy in Staffordshire and the obstacles involved would be jumping into ice cold water and also getting electrocuted. Also in January I will be doing the New Year day swim which I did last year and was very cold but tremendous fun. When I got home at 4pm I had a parcel waiting for me. I opened the parcel and the parcel was my remote control battery charger that I ordered from a company on EBay last Friday evening, I charged my Lipo battery for my remote control Car and made sure that the Lipo battery was in a special container pouch as Lipo batteries could possibly catch on fire.

18th September 2013

I was very excited at dinner-time at work as I received a phone call from one of my swimming friends asking me would I like to swim the Pier to Pier swim in Blackpool on Sunday 22nd September 2013. I was over-joyed with this news I have always wanted to swim offshore at Blackpool and now I have the opportunity to swim from Blackpool South Pier to the North Pier and I will be swimming a distance of 1.75 miles. After Tea I took my remote control car which is a FTX Vantage Buggy with a brushless motor and does 30mph. At New Brighton seafront where I come to play with my remote control car, it was very quiet on the playing fields at New Brighton. I played with my r/c Car on New Brighton Sea Front for a good 20 minutes and then I went to Starbucks cafe and had a nice cup of Coffee. Once I had my Coffee in Starbuck's I then went into Home and Bargain and got a packet of Twiglets and 2 bottles of Wychwood Ruby Ale to drink on the Friday Night while watching a Movie.

19th September 2013

I got the last of the sponsorship money that I have raised for the baby unit in Countess of Chester and then sent a Cheque by post to the Babygrow Appeal. I had enjoyed raising money for the Baby unit and I had amazing 6 mile swim on Saturday 14th September 2013 swimming down the River Dee. We had Tea at 5pm and then I had a shower using Original Source Lemon shower gel and then I had a wet shave using Real Shaving Company shaving gel and I am also still putting my anti-biotic cream on my Lip to get rid of the last of the Lip infection in the corner of my mouth. At 7pm me and Lee went to see the Formula one film called Rush that is set in the 1976 Formula one season against James Hunt and Nikki Lauder. The movie was very good and I enjoyed watching it. After the movie we made our way home and we talked about formula one cars that were driven in the Seventies era of formula one which included a six wheel formula one Car made by the company Tyrell and was a lovely coloured Blue.

20th September 2013

At 4pm I finished my intensive Relaxation drawing which is a drawing of me on a medical Breathing Ventilator with medical equipment attached to me at the Great Spa of Aurora. Once I had finished the Intensive relaxation drawing I looked at the drawing from a short distance and knew I put the right colours in it. There is a lot of Colour in all my drawings and I love using bright colours and enjoy using Coloured crayons. After completing my new drawing I emailed one of my swimming friends and asked them would any of them like to go for a night swim in Liverpool Docks on Monday 23rd September 2013. Dad had finished building the Wall in the small Garden next to the patio windows. Over the last couple of days I have been worrying about the Baby fish in the bottom pond as it would soon be October and the fish are too little to handle a very cold winter. Mum and Dad have decided to create a small tank in the summer house and I will feed them every day over the Winter Months. The summer house hasn't been used this Year because it has been used to Radiators.

21st September 2013

It was Saturday today I had got up earlier at 7.30am and did my next drawing for the Return to the Spa of Aurora, which was called Ashokan Farewell which is music instrumental piece composed by Jay Ungar 1982. The drawing has me playing a Violin to a Red Spotted Octopus and the piece of music I am playing in Ashokan Farewell. At 9am I went with Mum to follyfields Nursery at Eastam where we got some Winter Pansies for our wall Garden which we both look after.

At dinnertime I had Cheese on Toast and two Chocolate rice crispy cakes that Mum had made Yesterday. After dinner I looked at Smyth Toys Winter Catalogue and looked at the different themed Lego sets you could buy from Smyth Toys. Dad took me down to New Brighton sea-front where I played with my remote control Cars and Dad took his remote control dirt-bike which has a brushless motor in it. In the evening I got my swim Bag ready for the Blackpool swim that I was doing tomorrow afternoon. I hopefully I will be swimming from the South Pier to the North Pier, and I am very excited about the swim tomorrow.

22nd September 2013

We sat in the Beach patrol Land Rover driving to the South Pier at Blackpool. The Beach patrol lifeguards had given us a lift to the start of the swim which was the steps to the right of the South pier. At 12pm we entered the Water by the side of South Pier which was now coming to high tide.

There were 7 swimmers doing the Pier to Pier swim. The sea was quite choppy and was quite a struggle to get into the calmer deep water. Once we all got into deep water we started swimming towards the end of the middle Pier. Once we got to the end of the middle Pier we then swam past the middle Pier and then I could see the North Pier in my swim goggles, then we made our way to the North Pier and swum under the Pier to the awaiting slipway which was the finish of the Pier to Pier swim at Blackpool. After the swim we all went to the Promenade Cafe and I had a Cheese Burger with Chips and a filtered Coffee. At the Promenade cafe we all talked about how much fun the swim was and how the Sea was very choppy to swim in.

23rd September 2013

I made my way down the stone steps of Queen Dock and submerged myself into the cold water. It was 8:30pm at Night and me and two other swimmers had come to Queen Dock to do a Night Swim. Night Swimming is a lot of fun and is very exciting swimming in the Dark. As I entered the water I could see the streets lights reflecting off the water and how still the water looked. I got into the water and treaded water while the other two swimmers made their way into the Water. After they entered the Water we then set off swimming down the dock in the Dark. I couldn't really see much in my swim goggles but I could I see splashing in front of me from one of the other swimmer kick. We did 2 laps of Queen Dock and then we got out via the stone steps where we had left our bags. We got changed on a grass verge next to the Dock and then we had a drink of Coffee and I talked about Farmaggedon that one of my swim friends was coming too. Farmaggedon is an interactive Scare Attraction where scare actors jump out at you and scare you.

24th September 2013

It seems the whole World is now full of technology and smartphones. To be honest I enjoy my Android smartphone and I love playing Angry Bird. My Brother Lee was looking after me this week and he cooked Beef burger Batch and hash browns for Tea which I really enjoyed eating. In the evening I played with my Apple IPad and I am creating a musical universe with an application called Planetary. After playing with my apple iPad I then did some research on my new book I am writing that I am really excited about. At 9pm I had a wet shave and then I had a shower using

Original Source Shower Gel. After I got out of the shower I have started to notice that I am beginning to put on weight and I am not comfortable with my Body anymore.

I suppose the weight gain is to do with the medicine I have to take. I have looked at losing weight as I am taking on too much weight. I don't want to lose too much weight as my fat is useful while I am swimming in very cold water like a Seal.

25th September 2013

I was crying this afternoon as I was upset that the Open Water Swimming season is coming to an end. The Open Water swimming season is from April to September. There has been talk about extending the swimming season at Queen Dock, Liverpool to October 2013. But it is the same every year once we have the first frost the Open Water swimming sessions come to a close due to the water being too cold to swim in. unofficially we do polar Bear swimming in the Winter months and winter open water swimming is a lot of Fun. When you get into really cold water in January you get an invigorating surge of adrenalin which goes through your whole body. This evening I started work on my next drawing for the Great Spa of Aurora which is American Wild West Steam Locomotive from 1876. The carriage in the drawing will be the relaxation suite where I had been placed from being in the Intensive Relaxation Suite which closely resembled an Intensive care unit in a Hospital setting. For supper I had Prawn cocktail crisps and a Glass of Tizer pop and some chocolate after eating the prawn cocktail crisps.

26th September 2013

I arrived at Beau-tea rooms in Bromborough on the Wirral for 3:40pm. The Beau-tea room is a Beauty Salon that does my toenails for me and while I waited I looked at the pictures in a travelling Magazine. At 4pm the therapist ushered me into the Beauty parlour and then I took a seat in a nice comfy lounge chair and then the Therapist let my feet have a soak in a portable foot spa. Then the therapist took each of my feet in turn and cleaned and polished my toenails. After polishing my toenails the therapist asked me what colour I would like to have my toenails painted. I decided to go for a metallic Blue. The therapist coloured my toenails for me and then made a coffee for me and I drank my coffee and looked at the Holiday magazine while my Toenails dry. In the holiday magazine was 10 page spread about going on

Holiday to Japan. I would love to go to Japan for a holiday and I would visit the City of Kyoto and take a photograph of a Maiko which is an Apprentice Geisha. I would also try the Japanese hot Bath's which are called Onsen.

27th September 2013

Me and Lee had tea and then in the evening I set to work drawing a new picture of me Returning to the Great Spa of Aurora. The drawing I am working on is the Spa of Aurora Train station and then Train was a Locomotive from the American Wild West around about 1876. I draw the drawing in Pencil and then I go over Pencil drawing with Black Ink and then I add the Colour.

I like using Crayola wax crayons and coloured felt tips and coloured pencils. My favourite is using wax crayons and I use very Bright colours to make my drawings stand out. I finished the pencil sketch of the Spa of Aurora Train Station and then I had a shower for 9pm at night and then got changed into my Night Shirt and put my Blue dressing Gown on and my Red and White spotty Chef Hat on and then snuggled up on my Bed with Herbert my Toy T-rex and watched the Japanese Samurai Movie 13 Assassins. I had my medicine at 10pm and it relaxes me quite a lot and within half an hour I am fast a sleep with Herbert my cuddly Toy T-rex Dinosaur.

28th September 2013

When I got up 9:30am I saw that my bedroom was a mess and needed cleaning up and I had stuff all over the floor. First I started by having a Shower, brushed my teeth, and washed my glasses that I wear because my eye sight is not very good. After I had a shower I made my way to the kitchen and I had a filtered coffee and two round of toast. Once I had breakfast and took my morning medicine I then set to work cleaning my Bedroom. I washed my ornaments in my room in Bucket of hot soapy water with Stardrops liquid, I have two shelves in my bedroom. The first shelve has three ornamental Geisha about 15" high and are very Beautiful. My second shelve has a Lego unfinished technic crane and cuddly toys. On my walls in my Bedroom I have two Danelectro Guitars and have a 26" LCD television mounted on the Wall. Once I had cleaned my room I then washed my Car and made sure it was beautiful cleaned inside and out. For Tea I had oven baked Pizza with pepperoni which I really enjoyed eating, Lee my brother had 2 turkey burgers and oven chips with a cup of Tea.

29th September 2013

I didn't have a very good Night sleep as I woke up from a Nightmare about 4am in the morning, the nightmare was, I was being gassed in a Gas Chamber and then I woke up. I went downstairs and made myself a cup of Tea and then back to Bed with the cup of the tea and drunk my cup of Tea in Bed. After I drunk my cup of tea I tried to get back to sleep again and eventually had another sleep. I got up 10am and I realised I had missed the open Water swimming session at Queen Dock this morning. I was quite annoyed with myself as I wanted to go to this Open Water swimming session as official it is the last swim session of the season but I think the swim sessions at the Dock might be on throughout October as long as the temperature doesn't drop. In the afternoon me and my Brother cleaned the house up as Mum and Dad where coming home from there Caravan is North Wales. I cleaned the Bathroom and hoovered around the house. I also watered all the plants in the Garden using the Garden hosepipe.

30th September 2013

I got St Catherines Hospital in Birkenhead and made my way to the second floor to the inter-mediate suite for my appointment with ADHD Nurse. I was at St Catherines Hospital for a medicine review for my ADHD medicating. During the appointment I spent most of the time talking Farmaggedon Scare Attraction that one of my swimming friends was coming too. After ten minutes the Nurse was happy that my medication was stable and then she took my blood pressure. After Tea I looked on the internet at a new remote control Car that was coming out at the end of October called the Kyoshi Rage VE. I have booked two days off from work in October where me and Mum will be going to the Waterslide Park in Blackpool called the Sandcastle. We are going to the Sandcastle on the 10th October 2013 and the following day I am going on a Spa Day to Mottram Hall in Cheshire.
Then on the 12th October I am going white Water tubing at Llangollen in North Wales, where I will be going down the rapid on an inflatable rubber ring.

1st October 2013

I have begun a new month in my Diary, I have been looking forward to October and the Halloween Attractions that are come in this month Adventures. It had been a quiet day and before tea I did some writing outside. The Wind was blowing through the Garden and I had to hold my writing paper down while I wrote some new material for the return to the Great Spa of Aurora. I write with a Cross mason Pen which is a beautiful Pen to write with. At 5pm I fed the Baby fish in the bottom pond, the baby fish are growing at a good rate but I think Mum and Dad are going to create a fish tank in the summer house so they can survive the winter months. This evening looked on the internet to see when the new Sony PlayStation 4 is coming out. I think the release date is late November 2013. The Sony PlayStation 4 will be quite expensive on its launch. Later on at 8pm I put all of my Hotwheel toy Cars on the Dining table in rows of twenty. While playing with my Hotwheels collection I put my wizard cloak on. While putting my hotwheel cars on the dining room table I thought it would be great if I got myself a Pink Kimono and under Kimono.

Feminine side of Nicholas Robinson

I make no secret of the fact I am a Transvestite and I enjoy my Feminine side. The Female clothes I wear are very special. There are three costumes I wear when I am exploring my Feminine side, the first is the Japanese Geisha or Geiko. The second costume is an Indian Saree with Beads and the third costume is a 17th Century Georgian Dress with a Corset and matching wig. If you have read my book about my Adventures or if you are new to my World. I enjoy being laced into a Corset and when you are laced into a corset you get an amazing feeling of Euphoria. The Geisha costume is very similar to wearing a corset as Geisha's wear a thick band around there waist called a Obi which compresses your stomach in. when I become a geisha I put the white make-up and I put red lipstick on and use a Blue eye shadow. I have a real Geisha wig from Japan which is called a Katsura Wig with the make-up and costume for the Geisha takes about 2 hours to get into the Geisha costume and can only be worn for 1 or 2 hours as I get very hot in the Geisha Costume and I use a Paper fan to cool me down.

2nd October 2013

I got to New Brighton Seafront for about 3:40pm in the afternoon. I parked my Car on the seafront and then I made my way down a set of steps which are situated between the storm Wall on New Brighton Promenade. I got to the bottom of the steps and then I started walking on the Sand.

I had come to New Brighton Sea Front to wade in the small Lagoons on the Beach that the Tide leaves behind once the tide goes out. I came to a small lagoon and then I took my shoes and socks off and rolled my Jeans up and then entered the shallow lagoon. The water was cold but I enjoyed wading in salt water and love having sand between my Toes. While wading I felt a slight pinch on my little toe and realised that a Crab was trying pinch my Little Toe. I did a silent ouch that hunt and moved over to the other side of the lagoon. After about 10 minutes I got out of the Lagoon and dried my feet with a small towel that I took with me. Then I put my shoes and socks back on and then walked along the Beach and then climbed the steps back to my Car.

3rd October 2013

I arrived at Holistic Hands on Seabank Road , Wallasey for a full Body Massage. The therapist greeted me at the Door and she had a lovely smile to her. The Therapist was a lovely bubbly person and I enjoyed her company for the Hour long full body massage that I was having done to me.

The actual massage I had done to me is called a Hands Free Massage. The therapist uses her forearms for a powerful yet deeply relaxing massage. I really enjoyed this blissful massage experience and the therapist even massages my head and I fell in love with the therapist massaging my ears and I become very relaxed after my Head massage. The therapist finished with giving me a back massage using her forearms and she released a lot of tension in my back that had built up due to my demanding open water swimming season. The Therapist also does Hopi Ear Candling and includes a head massage and ear massage which i have now fell in love with. In the evening I listened to some music on my Ipod which was Led Zeppelin 'Whole Lot of Love'.

4th October 2013

I got home for 3:30pm and I played on the internet and did more research for the Book that I am writing. Mum cooked a meat Pie tonight and we had mash potato and Vegetables. I had not been well today and someone had the central heating on to maximum level at work and I was working in my T-shirt during the Day. This evening I am going to Farmaggedon a Scare Attraction in Liverpool. I have been a couple of times to this Scare Attraction and this Attraction is Genuine scary and I get terrified when I go through the haunted House. Chris one of my swimming friends is coming with me to Farmaggedon and I made up I have company while walking around this scare attraction. We arrived at the Scare Attraction and we took our place in the queue to enter the scare attraction. After 10 minutes we got to the entrance of the scare show and the lady put a wrist band around my wrist and then me and Chris entered the Scare Attraction. I didn't know what to expect as this Year Farmaggedon is for 18 Years old only.

I was absolutely terrified I was hiding behind a metal Oil Drum while two men with chainsaw's hovered above me and a third man with a chainsaw was also coming towards me. I was in the second scare house hiding behind a metal oil drum, eventually I came out from the back of the Oil drum and ran towards the exit of the second scare house where my friend Chris was waiting for me.

Once we completed the second scare attraction and then we took our place in the queue for the third and final Scare attraction Scare house. The queue was quite big for the final Scare attraction and we had to wait about 15 minutes to get to the entrance of the third scare house. The final scare house was called Psychosis and was full of Zombies and clowns and dark creatures from your worst Nightmares. In the middle of the last scare house there was a revolving walk way where I thought I was walking upside down. At the end of the last scare house was a scarecrow with a chainsaw that chased me around the farm and I was still scared from the second scare house. We got some photographs with some zombies and then made our way home.

5th October 2013

I got up for about 10am and it was Saturday morning and I had a great time last night at Farmaggedon and today was quite in respect of last night scare Adventures. In the afternoon I did a new drawing where I come to the Spa of Eusebius and I am greeted by one of the Therapists outside the doors of the Spa of Eusebius. While doing my drawing I listened to some classical music and made myself a cup of filtered coffee. Tea was fishfingers and chips with Red sauce and sweet pickles. In the evening I did some more drawings and sketches of my new Kimono set that is coming from Osaka, Japan. Later in the evening I did some research and I thought about new idea's for Adventures and wrote them down on a A4 piece of paper. I also played on my Sony Vita handheld Game console. I have got a Adventure game to play on my Sony Vita called Unchartered Golden Abyss where I go on Adventure to find Aztec Gold in the Jungles of Mexico. After playing on my Sony Vita game console I then watched a film and drank a pint of Wychwood Ruby Ale and packet of Monster Munch Pickled onion Crisps.

6th October 2013

Me and Dad went to Birkenhead North car park to play with Dad's remote control motorbikes and they are a lot of Fun. After about 20 minutes of playing with the remote control motorbikes we then went to New Brighton playing fields where I played with FTX r/c Buggy Car which I enjoyed playing with. In the afternoon Mum made Cheese on Toast for dinner-time. When I have Cheese on toast I like using red sauce and black pepper. After I had dinner I went looking for a Bumblebee in the back Garden, I love Bumblebee's I like the way they fly from one flower to another. I eventually found a Bumblebee and I watched it for ages as it hovered in the Air in the Autumn Sunshine. In the evening I watched a documentary about the American Wild west and the different Native American tribes that are in North America. One of the most favourite Native American Indians are Sitting Bull and Crazy Horse. Sitting Bull appeared in Buffalo Bill Wild West Show that toured around the World.

7th October 2013

I got to to Liverpool Central Library at 4:30pm and made my way to the Picton Library a circular Library within the Central Library. I haven't come to the Picton library to read a book, I have come to sit at a desk in the middle of the Picton Library and listen to White Shade of pale by Procol Harum through my Skullcandy headphones. I would love to play white shade of Pale through a speaker in the Picton ibrary as the acoustics would be amazing in a circular room with a dome.

After listening to white shade of Pale in the Picton Library with my Skullcandy headphones I then made my way back to the train station at Limestreet to get the New Brighton train home. When I got home I had tea with the family and then in the evening I watched an hour documentary about Apprentice Maiko which is an Apprentice Geisha. I was watching the documentary to watch how the Geisha put on there famous white make-up. I am quite excited about getting my new kimono from Osaka, Japan.

8th October 2013

I write with a Cross mason ballpoint Pen which is my Pen that I write my Books with. When I wrote my Autobiography called ' The Spiral Staircase '. Before I write a new book I put my Cross Pen next to my Bluetooth speaker to bring my Cross Pen to Life. To bring my Cross Pen to life I play "Battle Hymn of the Republic" by the Mormon Tabernacle Choir, located at the Church of Latter-day Saints. When I started this Diary I played " Battle hymn of the republic" to bring my cross Pen to life to bring my words alive. Mum has made me a cushion from a cross stitch Pattern of a Blue Car and it is very Beautiful. I spent the evening listening to 1960's rock and roll music and I have found an American themed Diner at Cheshire oaks outlet Village in Ellesmereport. I love the idea of having a Burger with fries and have mini jukebox next to me on the table. I was sad today and after tea I was crying by the fish pond while cuddling the Cat. The Open water swimming season is now coming to a close and my depression has started again.

9th October 2013

I was outside by the bottom Pond laying on the concrete floor at 2am in the morning. I had a paint brush in my hand and I was looking into the Night Sky with all the stars and I was pretending to paint the Night Sky with all it's Beautiful stars. While I was laying on the floor I heard someone open the back door and saw Mum and Dad with a torch looking around the Garden. I think they were looking for me as I wasn't in my bed. Mum and Dad found me very quickly and then I went back to Bed and cuddled Herbert my Cuddly T-Rex. When I look at the Night sky I always think of 1950's science Fiction movies and green eyed Aliens that are going to take over the World. Mum put my dressing Gown in the washing machine as I was laying on wet concrete when I was looking at the stars by the bottom Pond. It was quite in work today and this evening I got my swim bag ready to go to Blackpool Sandcastle Waterpark the next day.

10th October 2013

Me and Mum arrived at the Sandcastle Waterpark in Blackpool Promenade at 10:30am and I was really excited about going on the waterslides and the Blackpool Sandcastle had two new waterslides called Aztec Falls and Montazooma. We got changed in the changing rooms and then we made our way to the waterpark. The Sandcastle is a wash with lots of colours and I started on a vertical drop slide called sidewinder which I really enjoyed the vertical drop waterslide. After going on the sidewinder slide I went on the Aztec falls and found myself in an Alien Spacebowl and then dropped through a hole in the middle of the space bowl. Inside the spacebowl there was flashing lights and was quite amazing swirling around inside the spacebowl. I also went on Montazooma slide which was very fast. In the meantime Mum had fell in love with the Water Rapids called ushi-gushi River Creek and Mum went around the creek 10 times. I went on the waterslides a lot of times and I enjoyed the thrills of the twist and turns of the waterslides and I was very Happy.

11th October 2013

I sat beside the pool at Mottram hall and it was a very beautiful Pool with Blue small tiles. To the side of Mottram Hall Pool was a steam room and Sauna. On the far side of the swimming pool which led outside where there was a hot-tub that I decided to try. I put my towel on one of the Sun loungers outside and then just with my swimming trunks on I got into the outside hot-tub. The outside hot-tub was a lot of fun as it was raining but I was nice and warm in the hot-tub. At 1pm I went for Dinner which was fresh made orange Juice and a Chicken Wrap with salad which I enjoyed eating. At 2pm I went for my treatments which was a 30 minute Back and shoulder Massage and a express Facial. I really enjoyed my massage treatment as the therapist massaged my tail-bone which really relaxed me. After the massage I was given an express facial and then the therapist took me to the relaxation room where I had a nice sleep and then I had a nice hot shower and got changed and then made my way home.

12th October 2013

I was really depressed today and sat on the floor of my Bedroom crying and I was very upset and had floods of tears streaming down my face. I had a hand held mirror that I had on the floor beside me and I looked at myself in the hand held mirror and I saw a very sad person. I had completed my 3 year Adventure from February 2010 to May 2013 and at the end of the three Year Adventure I was to become an Angel but it never happened. I have been very sad all day and kept looking at myself in the hand held mirror hoping that my smile would return. Towards the end of the day I took one final look in the handheld Mirror and I found a smile looking back at me. At 10pm I took my bedtime medicine and then I got into Bed and cuddled up with Herbert my cuddly toy T-Rex and watched a film for half an hour and then I fell a sleep.

13th October 2013

There was a cold wind blowing on Queen Dock this morning. I stood on the slipway with my feet submerged into the Water. The Water was cold this morning, after a couple of minutes of my feet submerged in the water I put my Goggles down and waded into the Water and then the coldness of the water engulfed my body and I felt a glow of warmth in my Heart. After a couple of minutes treading water I got into my head into swim mode and then I swum over a mile around the course that is laid out for swimmers in Queen Dock, Liverpool. I completed my cold water swim and then when I got out I wrapped a towel around myself and then put my woolly bobble hat on as I like to keep my head warm when I get out of the water. I had a shower in the Changing room and got changed into my clothes. I love swimming this time of year it is very invigorating and I enjoy my tingle on my back that the cold water produces.

14th October 2013

I got home 3:30pm and there was two Parcel's waiting for me from Osaka, Japan. I took the 2 parcels from Japan to my Bedroom and I opened the parcels up in my Bedroom. The Parcels where my 2 kimono's that I won on Ebay. The first of the two Kimono's was a jupan which is the under Kimono which was very beautiful. The second parcel was the main kimono which was a stunning Pink and matched well with the under kimono. I have a Red Obi which is the waistband that wraps around the kimono and it matches the two new Kimono's in colour very well. I put the two new Kimono's in my wardrobe and then I dusted my Ornaments my Bedroom. On my second shelf I have a Lego Technic Crane that I still haven't finished yet. I dusted everything in my room including my LCD television and my Sony Playstation 3. Later in the evening I watched Ghostbusters with the Ghostbusters Car Ecto-1, which is a very cool Car. I love the Ghostbusters Film and Ghostbusters 2 is alright.

15th October 2013

I went with my Brother Lee and Mum to the giant Tesco Superstore at Bidston Moss. The store is very big and there is even an escalator to a second level where the Technology section is and I enjoy looking at the Ipod speakers. In my Bedroom I have a Panasonic Bluetooth speaker which I enjoy listening to my Music through. After going to Tesco's I looked at the new Hex bugs nano V2 bugs that can climb and can even go upside down and twist. Hex bugs are great and I love the Habitats that you can get for the Hex bugs nano V1 and the V2 bugs. The hex bugs nano V2 are the latest toys from Innovation first toy company. I took my medicine at 10pm and then I got into Bed and wrote a few idea's down for my Book that I am writing. After about 10 minutes of writing down some idea's I had a packet of Seabrook Prawn cocktail crisps with a glass of Tizer pop and watched a documentary about building the biggest ship in the World which is a Container vessel. At 11pm I switched off my television and had a good night sleep.

16th October 2013

I love Aviation and the freedom of flight, I had flown in a Gyrocopter a kind of small helicopter, Microlight a hanglider with an engine. I have been in a stunt plane over the skies of Blackpool which was a lot of fun. The Microlight flight was very similar to Da Vinci Glider and I very much enjoyed the Microlight experience. This morning I ordered a Leatherman Wingman multi-tool and I got it from amazon.com and I got the Leatherman tool at a good price with free super saver delivery. When I got home for tea I found that Mum had made mash potato and chicken which I really enjoyed eating. The desert was fairy cakes with white icing, and went well with a nice Cup of Tea. After Tea I cleaned the Guinea pig cage out and made sure the family pet Guinea Pig called Squeeky had fresh hay and straw, and filled his water bottle up to make sure Squeeky had water to drink. After cleaning the Guinea pig I cuddled the family Cat called Jessica. The Cat loves being cuddled and like chasing my mini remote control car.

17th October 2013

I received a Parcel on the 9th October 2013 and the content of the parcel was Japanese bondage rope. This evening I was with Mistress Serenity and I was having my first experience of Japanese Bondage Rope. I was quite nervous at first but the Mistress reassured me that this was going to be a good experience. The Mistress asked me to take all my clothes off and I did as the Mistress commanded and took off all my clothes. It didn't bother me at all being naked in front of the Mistress. Once I was naked Mistress Serenity started wrapping the Japanese Bondage rope around me and created knots within the Rope. Before long I was lying on the floor tied up in Japanese Bondage Rope and I felt Euphoria go through my Body and being held in bondage by the rope releases a lot of energy and tension that I didn't know was there. Once the mistress untied me from my bondage rope I humbly thanked her for experience of being place in Rope Bondage.

18th October 2013

This evening I went indoor swimming at the Local Swimming baths. They had two lanes roped off for Lane swimming. The first lane was for slower swimmers and the second swim lane was for the faster swimmers. Both swimming lanes where full of Breastroke swimmers I got myself ready and started swimming in the faster lane. I am a very modest person and respect other swimmers in the swim lane with me. However I do have a Big toe fetish, so when I swim up behind someone and see there big toe in the water I try and grab it, as all I see through my goggles is the Big toe wriggling in the Water. When I grab the swimmers big toe in front of me they usually stop and ask me what am I doing and I tell them I have a big toe fetish and then they start laughing. I swum 70 lengths tonight and I really enjoyed the swim indoors. I haven't swum indoors since March 2013 as I like swimming in Open Spaces and enjoy swimming in cold water.

19th October 2013

I arrived at Eccleston ferry for about 8pm and parked my Car in the Car park. Eccleston ferry is a small Village on the outskirts of Chester and is a beautiful place to swim. I was meeting 3 other swimmers tonight to do a Full Moon swim. The other swimmers arrived after me and we had a talk in the Car park and then we got changed ready for the Night Swim up the River Dee. At 8:30pm we made our way into the Water at Eccleston ferry, each of us had a glow stick attached to the back of our goggles so we could see each other as we swam up the River. It was slightly cold when I got into the River Dee and when I got in I found the River Dee to be very tranquil and very quite. All I could hear was the splashing of the water with us the Swimmers getting into the River Dee. Once we got in we started our 1km swim up the River Dee and we swam in complete Darkness with no light Pollution and we had a clear view of the Full moon and the stars of the Night Sky.

20th October 2013

I looked in the Attic and I was looking for the dark Red material that I had bought to make my Wizard costume. I found the material that I was looking for in the Attic and instantly knew that this was the colour for my Wizard costume. I spent the afternoon designing and sketching my wizard costume on Paper and wrote down what materials I would need to make the Wizard costume. I did a lot of sketches and decided on one of my Wizard costume sketches. I am going to enjoy making my Wizard costume for the 7th Age of Magic which starts on the 2nd January 2014. at 10pm I took my Medicine and then went to my bedroom and got my Stethoscope out from my Chest of draws and then I placed the stethoscope on the left side of my Chest and listened to the sound of my Heart. I fell into a blissful sleep listening to my Heart beating and pumping blood around my Body. The Magic of the Heartbeat is very Beautiful.

21st October 2013

I parked my car at the Water-sport Centre at Queen Dock for my swimming friend to arrive. It was 8pm at Night and I had arranged to do a Night swim in Queen Dock, Liverpool. I had brought my wetsuit with me tonight as the water was going to be colder then what the temperature was in the Summer months. My swimming friend arrived and we talked a few minutes about future swimming events and then we got changed. We got in via the stone steps at the end of Queen Dock, and the water temperature wasn't that bad as I thought the water was going to be a lot colder. The lights of the Water-sport Centre was still on, so we decided to swim in the first half of the dock away from the lights of the water-sport Centre. I love swimming at Night as it has more of an edge feeling about it and swimming is very Tranquil.

22nd October 2013

I got to Costa Coffee in Liverpool one at 6pm at Night. I got myself a medium size Coffee and sat down in a plush chair and waited for my friend to arrive. My friend is a Lady from Mongolia and she is a really Lovely Lady. My friend arrived and I got her a Coffee and then we sat down and talked about Her recent visit back to Mongolia and how much she enjoyed her Holiday in Mongolia. My friends name is Erdene and Erdene had brought her Ipad with her to show me some Beautiful photographs of the scenery of Mongolia and the photographs where amazing. We had a really nice talk about the Holiday in Mongolia and then 6:40pm we walked to James Street Train Station and we said our Goodbye's and I made my way home on the train and I looked out the Train window and saw that there was not much light outside and it was very Dark.

23rd October 2013

I sat on the Dock Wall looking at the half sunken Ship that is in the Dock near the four bridges, Birkenhead. While I sat on the Dock Wall I decided to see if I could get to the Bow mast of the half sunken ship. The half sunken ship is called Sarsia and was a marine biology research vessel and how it came to be half sunk in Birkenhead docks, I have no idea!

I took a slight jump from the Dock wall and I made it to the rusted side of Sarsia Ship. I could hear the ship making strange noises and then I made my way to the Bow mast and then climbed the Bow mast and felt good about myself on achieving this task. Then I realised I had to make my way back to the Dock Wall. I sat on the rusting Hull of the Ship trying to figure out how I was going to get back to the Dock Wall. The Sun beamed down on my face and enjoyed sitting on this half sunken Ship with Sun Shining on me.

24th October 2013

I received a Phone call at 7pm and I got invitation to look at the Wormhole tunnels in New Brighton and I was asked could I come tonight at 8:30pm and I was told to bring a Torch. I arrived at a House in new Brighton at 8:15pm and I knocked on the door of the House and a Man greeted me at the Door and invited me into his Back Garden, at the far end of the Man Garden there was a door way which had a set of stone steps that lead to Cave of Tunnels that was very impressive. We went around the Tunnels with torches and slightly eerie as you could imagine smugglers using these tunnels and I think these tunnels are Haunted. The Man showed me the tunnels and I thought the tunnels where amazing. After a good half hour tour of the Wormholes tunnels the Man lead me back up the stone steps and I then thanked him for the Tour of New Brighton Wormholes Tunnels.

25th October 2013

I sat on my Bed and played my Danelectro Guitar and I was learning how to play 'whole lot of Love' by the band Led Zeppelin. I like playing Danelectro Guitars and I have a Danelectro Wild thing electric Guitar and Danelectro Convertable which is a Semi-accoustic Guitar. I also have a Danelectro Honeytone mini amplifier which has overdrive on it. I enjoy playing my Guitar and I got the rhythm of the Led Zeppelin song I was learning. In the evening I watched a Horror movie called the Evil Dead 2013 which is a remake the 1980's horror movie The Evil Dead. The horror movie was very scary and I hid under my Duvet at the scary bits, and while I watched the Movie I ate Golden Wonder salt and vinegar crisps. I took my Medicine at 10pm and then I snuggled up into my Bed and thought I had a real Adventurous week this week and it was Halloween next week.

26th October 2013

I waited in Foyer of the Liver-Building for the tour of the Liver-building rooftop to see the iconic Liverbirds that sit on top of the Liver-building. There was ten of us on the tour to see the Liverbirds. I went with the others that where on the tour to the lifts to go to the roof of the Liver-building. We got to the roof and I was nearly blown away by the wind. The Liverbirds statues where very impressive and when your close to them they are quite big Statues. I enjoyed seeing Liverpool from the roof of the Liver-building and I saw all the Ships in the River Mersey. After about 25 minutes we went back to the lifts and went back to the Ground floor. When I got outside I looked up towards the Liverbirds and thought to myself I have just been to the roof of the Liver-building and I was very happy to be close to the Liverbird Statues and look upon the River Mersey.

27th October 2013

I got to the Dock for a swim at 10am and then I realised the clock's have gone back and it was 9am in the morning and I had come for a swim earlier and it was raining as well. I got changed into my swimming trunks and then I made my way too Queen Dock slipway and first I put my feet in the Water and I found it wasn't as cold as I thought it was going to be, but to be honest I have been swimming in open water for over ten years and my senses have gone numb for swimming in cold water too long. I got into the Water and then I swam 2 miles which is 7 circuits of the Dock. While I was swimming I could see the bottom of the Dock, then I realised how cold the water really was, as it only when the water is cold can you see to the bottom of the dock. I had a surprise for me after the swim, Lorna had brought me a Fat Willy Phone pouch from her family holiday in Cornwall.

28th October 2013

On the way home from Work I called into the Electronic shop Maplin's to get myself a Mini SAD lamp, Seasonal Affective Disorder. Then I made my way home and wondered what the SAD lamp was going to be like. Mum had cooked Tea which was Mash Potato, Carrots and Fish. After Tea I tried the SAD lamp out on the dining room table, while I looked on the internet. I spent a good hour sitting in front of the intense light coming from the SAD lamp and I quite enjoyed the experience. I started a new drawing for the Great Spa of Aurora which is me in a Roman Toga at the Spa of Eusebius looking at the Tree of Light. Mum asked me if I am going to do a Christmas Acrylic Painting, I quite like the idea of doing a Christmas Painting and making Christmas Cards for the Family. I took my Medicine at 10pm and watched television until I fell a sleep with Herbert my cuddly toy T-rex Dinosaur.

29th October 2013

I took my seat in the Anglican Cathedral in Liverpool to listen to the Choir sing Sou Gan. The Choir sang Sou Gan and was very beautiful to listen to. The Choir voices filled the whole Cathedral and the surround Sound was very good. When the Choir had finished singing Sou Gan I had a tear in my Eye. Once the Choir finished singing Sou Gan, I made my way to the Cathedral exit content that I heard the Choir sing Sou Gan. The cold Air of late October engulfed me as I exited the Cathedral and made my way outside. I made my way down Bold Street and the sweet aroma of Coffee bean lured me into Costa Coffee for a lovely filtered coffee. I sat in Costa coffee and drank my filtered coffee and looked at my Android phone which has the family Cat Jessica as my Wallpaper and Jessica is a very cuddly Cat. I drunk my Coffee and made my way to the Train Station.

30th October 2013

Me and Mum took our seats in the Cafe area of Perch Rock Fort and waited for our Group to enter the Creep Scare Attraction that was at the Perch Rock Fort in New Brighton. I had never been to this Scare Attraction before and I wondered what it was going to be like. The Creep Scare attraction was more of a play as the group we where in moved around the Fort. The Scare Attraction was more like ghost hunting with Scare Actors taking part of Ghosts and Evil Spirits. The Creep Scare attraction was enjoyable and at times a little bit scary. We got home for 9:30am and I took my Medicine at 10pm and then watched a Horror film. Sometimes the best Adventures is snuggling up in Bed with Lemonade and a packet of Pickled Onoin Monster Munch Corn snacks. I enjoyed watching the Horror film, I like watching the classic hammer horror films with Christopher Lee playing Dracula with Blood Sucking Fangs.

31st October 2013

I stood in the queue for the Pepsi Max big one a very tall Rollercoaster in Blackpool. I had come to Blackpool Pleasure Beach to come on the Thrill Rides and the Pleasure Beach was called Vampire Beach and there was Scare Actors roaming around the Pleasure Beach. I took my place in one of the Cars for the Rollercoaster Ride, the ride started and I soon found myself going upwards towards the top of the Rollercoaster. Once the Car-train had reached the top of the rollercoaster there was a sharp downwards turn plunging back to the ground level. I enjoyed riding on the Pepsi Max Big One. My other favourite ride this evening was the Valhalla Ride, you could say I got slightly wet on the Valhalla ride as the ride is a Viking Longship which is like a Log fume ride. The Valhalla ride goes into the Viking Underworld and takes you on a breathe taking finally that has to be done to be enjoyed, I had a Great evening in Blackpool Pleasure Beach.

1st November 2013

The first of November had arrived and I was now completed half of the 4 months diary that I am writing. It was a medium Day today at Work and this evening I ordered a Longboard which is an over-sized Skateboard. What I didn't realise is that the Longboard Skateboard is 5ft long and wouldn't fit in the back of my Car. I have had to send an email to cancel the order for the 5ft Longboard. I have fell in Love with the idea of Land Paddle boarding on New Brighton Promenade which has a concrete strip where I have seen people with paddle boards using a stick which extends to about 6ft in Length. After cancelling the order I went to my Bedroom and watched a film called the Conjuring which is a Horror movie and I decided to try a bottle of Beer which is Budweiser route 66 Beer. The Beer had a nice taste to it and I enjoyed drinking Budweiser route 66 Beer. I fell a sleep about 11pm and got woken up by my Dad at 9am to go to Liverpool City Centre to look at the Musical Instruments Shops.

2nd November 2013

Myself and my Dad went to Liverpool City Centre this morning to go to the Music Shops as Dad wanted a Ukulele. We went on the Train to Liverpool from Birkenhead North station and it was the first time Dad had been on the Train for a long time. We got off the Train at James Street and made our way into the City centre to Dawsons Music Shop. Dawsons Music Shop was a very large Musical Instrument shop in Williamson Street. Dad chose a nice Ukulele and then when we got home he gave the Ukulele to Mum as he wanted the Ukulele for a Christmas present. In the afternoon me and Mum put the baby fish into a plastic container and then put the Fish in the Plastic container into the Summer House. Hopefully the frost wont get to the babyfish as the babyfish are still tiny. In the evening I did some more drawing for the return to the Spa of Aurora, my latest drawing is called the Tree of Light and I have put a lot of Bright Colours into this drawing.

3rd November 2013

I got into the cold water of the Dock for 10am, amazingly enough the Open water swimming sessions are still going and we are now in November 2013. The water now is getting very cold. I enjoyed the swim this morning and I did 5 laps this morning, just under 2 mile. The shower was nice and hot and brought much needed warmth to my body. It had been raining all morning and stopped about 1pm in the Afternoon. In the afternoon I climbed Grannies Rock at the Breck which is abandoned Quarry in Wallasey that has a rock about 20 feet high in the middle of the Quarry. I sat on the top of Grannies Rock and felt the wind blowing in my Hair. I sat on top of the rock for a good 20 minutes and then I climbed down and walked the half a mile distance back home. While walking back home I listened to music on my Sony Walkman phone and I sang along to the Music.

4th November 2013

I was on the internet this evening and I was bidding for a Goonies treasure Key replica from the movie Goonies. I was out-bided at the last moment and never won the replica Goonies treasure key. I was looking forward to tomorrow Night as me and Mum where going to see the circus of horrors Show at the Floral Pavilion in New Brighton. After being out-bided on Ebay I did some research on a Day trip to Lapland in December and I got very excited. After playing on the internet I did some sewing on my Mermaid costume that I am making. I love the idea of becoming a real Mermaid. I have looked on the Website at Waterproof make-up, I like the idea of Blue eyeliner that is waterproof. I think eyeliner is highly erotic and I love wearing eyeliner and I like a Women applying eyeliner to my eyelids, I find it very enjoyable. Unfortunately I am not very good at applying make-up to my face and usually have the make-up all over the bathroom.

5th November 2013

Watching someone get sawn in half on a stage is a unique experience, your constantly trying to figure out how the magic was done, but you can never figure it out. I was at the Circus of Horrors and I was being well entertained. I watched a Contortionist shoot a bow and Arrow with her feet which was amazing to watch. The Circus of Horrors finished at 9:30pm and then me and Mum made our way to the Car Park by New Brighton Marine Lake and found that the Car park was very dark. I had a mini Maglite with me and I put the torch on to find our way back to the Car. While trying to find the Car with my torch I could feel the cold night breathing onto my Lungs. We found my Car and then we made our way home and I took my medicine for 10pm and then watched the Cartoon Ice Age 3 dawn of the Dinosaurs which was very funny. I fell a sleep at 11pm with a chuckle in my Heart.

6th November 2013

I tried my first pair of UGG Boots on today in the UGG Shoe Shop at Cheshire Oaks outlet Village in Ellesmereport. Believe it or not but they sell Men's UGG Boots. I found the UGG Boots to be very comfy and I now understand why a lot of Women enjoy wearing UGG Boots. I had a walk around Cheshire Oaks and nothing really interested me apart from Lindt Chocolate Shop and the Cadbury's outlet Shop. I am very much a Chocolate lover and I can eat a Giant Cadbury Diary milk block of Chocolate in one go. I am very partial to a Chocolate Eclair. In the evening I ordered a Drop down Longboard called the Atom from a online Skateboarding Shop. I looked at Remote control Models Cars on the internet and I have seen a remote control Car that I like. The Remote Control that I have seen is a HPI Chevelot Camero which is the Robot Bumblebee from the Film Transformers. I thought about ordering the R/C Car for December, and I love the Robot Bumblebee from the film Transformers that transforms into a Yellow Camero 2010 model.

7th November 2013

I was quite excited today as I had booked a floatation tank therapy session for the 14th December 2013. In the floatation tank I will be floating in concentrated salt, and will be like floating in the Dead Sea. I got home for 4pm and found that my Skateboard had arrived and Mum and Dad told me I would be getting the Longboard Skateboard for Christmas as well as the Kahuna Paddle Stick. I was made up I would be getting the Longboard for Christmas. This evening I have started a new drawing for the return to the Spa of Aurora, the drawing I am doing this evening is me getting a massage and the therapist is using Cactus Leafs on my Back. A Cactus massage is actually real and the therapist uses Tequila to massage into the Skin and lay Cactus leafs on the Patient back. I had a lot of fun this evening drawing a therapist massage me with Cactus leafs. I love using a lot of colour but I couldn't figure out what Colour a Cactus is.

8th November 2013

I knocked on the solid wood Arch door and I was greeted by an Elderly Man in a dark Blue Suit. The gentleman showed me in and then shut the Arched wooden door behind us. The Gentleman led me to a stone walled room which had a small wooden table in the corner of the room with a highly decorated Metal cup on the small wooden table. I looked at the decorated Metal Cup for a good 10 minutes and thought the Metal Cup to be very Beautiful. I was very happy to look at the Metal Cup and felt honoured to be in the same room of this Metal Cup. After I looked at the Metal Cup we made our way back to arched wooden door and I said my goodbye's to the Gentleman who showed me the Decorated Metal Cup. Sometimes the path to enlightenment can be found in the Open Air and not a Reign of Fire that Scorched this Once Beautiful Building. I made my way home content that I had now made my Heart Pure and I had let Colour back into my life to create the love of Pureness.

9th November 2013

I poured the filtered Coffee into my Cup and took my morning medicine which consists of 4 tablets. I sat by the Patio window in the Dining Room and watched the Birds feeding on all the Bird feeders scattered around the garden. I had now completed the Mermaid costume and I was looking forward to trying the Mermaid costume out. While I was drinking my coffee, Dad came into the House from his Workshop and asked could I get a Feeler Guage from the Shops in Liscard. I had never heard of a Feeler Guage and I went to Liscard to try and see if I could purchase such a device.

I eventually bought a Feeler Gauge in the towns DIY store called Howells. Dad wanted a Feeler Guage to set up his Guitar and drop the action on his Guitar. In the afternoon I did some drawing for the Return to the Great Spa of Aurora. In the evening I played on the internet and listened to Music on my Ipod. I am still looking for a Goonies Treasure Key on the Ebay Auction Site.

10th November 2013

I sat on the edge of the jetty at Queen Dock with my feet dangling in the Water and thought to myself 'what a really good swim season I have had. After a couple of minutes thinking about the swim season, I lowered myself into the Water. The Water temperature was a cool 7 oC and I felt the cold snap as I entered the Water. I did 2 laps of the Dock this morning and afterwards I got a hot shower in the Watersport Centre changing room. In the afternoon I helped Mum put all the bird food out on the Bird feeders around the Garden. There is a flock of Sparrows that comes to the Bird feeders in the back Garden and is fun to watch the Birds eating. In the evening I looked at the Planet Saturn through my Telescope, I enjoyed looking at Saturn and it's many rings, it is very Beautiful Planet to look at. I sat on a chair in the back Garden and took in the beauty of the Night Sky, and I looked at the different stars in the Night Sky using a round Phillips Plansphere.

11th November 2013

I sat at the Bar wearing my Marie Antionette Costume and my Wig was a women Georgian period and the wig went well with my costume. I was at a radical Desires Night at a BDSM club on Merseyside and I was really enjoying myself, I had come to the Bar to get myself a Coffee. I was given a filtered Coffee and I carefully drunk my Coffee so I didn't smudge my Red lipstick that I had on. Later in the night I had a play on the swing with a mirror in front of it so I can see myself as Marie Antionette. I had a great night being Marie Antoinette and before I left the club I took off all my make-up as I had put a nice foundation on and it took me a few minutes to get all the make-up off. I got home just after mid-night and I took my medicine and then I snuggled up in Bed with my cuddly Dinosaur, I thought how great I looked in the Georgian Period Gown and I had a corset on as well. I had to use a fan all night as the Gown and Corset is very hot to wear for a long time.

12th November 2013

It was 1am in the morning and I was Ghost hunting at Newsham Park Hospital in Liverpool. I was using a torch in the Dark Psychiatric Ward at Newsham Park Hospital and I could hear knocking noises from the punishment cupboards. What did freak me out to a degree was coming across a room that read ECT Therapy written on the door. I opened the door to the ECT room and was greeted by a operating table in the middle of this medical room, and the operating table had some formidable restraint straps where someone would be strapped down to the table and given electric shock treatment. The ECT medical room looked very menacing and while I was standing in this room I heard a noise as if someone or something had switched a machine on in this room I was standing in. I decided to leave the ECT therapy room and get back to the make shift reception desk where the Ghost Hunting staff where pouring Coffee for everyone.

13th November 2013

I sat in the steam room at the local health centre and I was slightly tired from my Adventures over the last two days and I was enjoying relaxing in the steam room. After a good 20 minutes being in the steam room I headed over to the cold plunge Pool. I got into the Cold plunge pool and found it very invigorating. I was in the cold plunge pool for a good couple of minutes and I got use to the temperature of the water. I realised there was a queue forming to use the cold plunge pool as I was hogging the pool. I got out of the cold plunge pool and then got into a nice hot-tub for a good long soak. While in the hot-tub I thought about what it would be like going in a yellow submarine that does tours in Tenerife (the Canary Island). I have fell in love with the idea of going on a Adventure holiday to Tenerife doing Scuba Diving, Surfing and most importantly going on Waterslides. There are two Waterparks in Tenerife, one is called Siam Waterpark and the second waterpark is called Aqualand, I do Love Waterslides!.

14th November 2013

I arrived at the Dark forest in Staffordshire for the last of this years Scare Attractions. The Scare attraction I had come to this evening was called the Woodlands of Terror and I would be using blank firing Assault rifle and the purpose of the evening was to search and destroy Werewolves.

At 10pm I joined the group I was in for the safety briefing and lecture on how to use the semi-automatic rifles. Then at 10:30pm we where ready to set out into the Woods to search for Werewolves. This Scare attraction was very much like the Film Dog Soldiers and the Werewolves looked very realistic in fact they looked too realistic for my liking. It was fun firing the semi-automatic rifle at the Werewolves in the Woods. One of the Werewolves came very close to me and at first I thought the Werewolf was going to bite me. This was a very scary attraction and the whole experience lasted over two hours and I was being chased by Werewolves.

15th November 2013

A man in a high visible jacket told me where to park my Car. Myself, Mum and my Brother Lee have come to Grosvenor Garden Centre Christmas Farmer's Market. I was lucky enough to find a Car parking space as a lot of people had come to this event. At the entrance to the Garden Centre they had a artificial Snow machine which was a lot of fun. The atmosphere in the Garden Centre was very magical as it is amazing when there is a lot of people it creates a really good atmosphere. The Farmer's market was good, and I found a stall that sold all different kinds of Chocolate and different Fudges. I treated myself to some Fudge and then I realised I had lost my Mum and my Brother Lee in the Crowd. I eventually found Lee and Mum, Mum was buying a Cactus Plant that she had chosen. After Mum got her Cactus we looked at all the different Christmas Tree decorations that was on offer. We even went for a coffee in the Coffee Shop and met Father Christmas with a pair of Sunglasses on.

16th November 2013

I got out of Bed full of excitement today as I was going Go-Karting this afternoon at a Go-karting track in Ellesmereport. The morning came and went and it was soon afternoon, and time to try Go-karting for the first time. The staff at the Go-karting gave me a set of Racing overalls to put on as well as a Crash Helmet. Once I was given the safety gear I was shown a Go-kart and it's layout.

The staff helped me get into the Go-kart as they are very low the Ground and I am having trouble with my Knee's. Once I got in the Go-kart I pressed my foot on the Accelerator and promptly crashed into a Tyre Wall. My first experience in a Go-kart and I end up crashing into a Tyre Wall.
I eventually got the hang of driving the Go-kart and I had a lot of fun driving around the Go-karting track. I got up to a good speed as well, these Go-karts are basically pocket rockets and are a lot of fun. By the end of the session my Knee's had become quite painful.

17th November 2013

I swam towards the slipway at Queen Dock and I realised that this was the last cold water swimming session this year. I felt a sadness in my Heart as I approached the slipway as I like hundreds of Open Water Swimmers around the World love swimming outdoors and indoor swimming in nowhere near as good as swimming long distance in Open Water. A part of me didn't want to get out of the Water as in my own mind I didn't know whether I would see the Open water again as I am Scared of my Winter Depression that last year took a heavy Toll on me. The truth is my depression is very severe and I don't know whether I am going to make it through the Winter months of 2013/2014. I eventually got out of the Water and then made my way to the Hot showers and I warmed myself up under the Shower. After I got changed I walked to my Car with a tear in my eye and the knowing that my Swim Goggles had now become Dry for the Winter season. I drove Home silently with tears in my eyes.

18th November 2013

Mistress Serenity explained to me what was going to happen to me. I had been invited to try a Vacuum Bed where a plastic sheet is put over your entire body and you breathe through a tube that has been created in the Plastic Sheet. Mistress Serenity told me to undress and I did as instructed and took all my clothes off as the Mistress is not a Shy Lady. Then I was told to lay on a make-shift Bed face up and then the Mistress lay the plastic sheet over my Body and then the mistress put the breathing tube into my Mouth and told me to breathe through the tube. Then the Mistress sealed me into this Vacuum Tomb and then to my surprise I could hear the sound of a vacuum cleaner and then I realised that the vacuum cleaner was connected to this Plastic Bed. Soon I couldn't move my Body as my attire body was in total vacuum suction and it was a Marvellous feeling. I breathed through the breathing tube while the Mistress caressed my Body as I lay there in Delight.

19th November 2013

I waited at the reception desk at the climbing Wall in Liverpool for one of my Swimming friends that was going to show me how to Rock Climb. My friend arrived a couple of minutes after me and then I rented some climbing gear from the Climbing Wall centre. Once I put my harness on I was then ready to tackle the Climbing Wall. I started off on a beginners Rock climbing Wall and I found it hard at first to grip the Wall to climb the Wall. After a good 20 minutes I eventually got the hang of Rock Climbing and then I tried climbing on the main Wall, which was a lot of fun. Towards the end of the Rock Climbing evening I decided to try the Rock face in the middle of the Climbing Centre to see of I could climb to the Top. I tried on numerous occasions to get to the top of the Rock face but in the end I realised I wasn't experienced enough and was exhausted from trying to climb this Rock face. I also tried the Climbing wall Cafe, where I got myself a Coffee and a Cake.

20th November 2013

Me and Mum went to visit Costco a Wholesale Warehouse on the Dock Road, Liverpool. When we entered the Warehouse we where amazed on how big Costco was. The Costco warehouse sold everything you could ever want and it took us a good 3 hours to get around the whole of the wholesale Warehouse. While at the Costco warehouse we visited the onsite Cafe for a Cheeseburger and a cup of Coffee. I enjoyed looking around the wholesale warehouse and I did purchase a few things. In the afternoon I fed the baby fish that we have in the summer house. Some of my swimming Friends told me it was snowing Yesterday in some parts of Britian. In the evening Me and Dad went to see the Film Gravity at the Cinema in 3D. The film Gravity is about 2 Astronauts that float into Space and I thought the film was very good. I love the idea of going into space as I have been brought up on science fiction films. The film finished at the Cinema in New Brighton at 10:30pm and then we made our way Home. I went to my Bedroom when we got home and set my Alarm clock for 5:30am, so my alarm clock would ring and wake me up.

21st November 2013

I stood at the Gates of Wallasey Cemetery and pressed start on my Ipod to listen to Ennio Morricone 'Ectascy of Gold' from the film soundtrack the Good, The Bad and the Ugly. The Music started and then I opened the gate to the Cemetery and started running in different directions around the Graveyard and as the Music got faster, so did my running and I was enjoying running around the Cemetery listening to music from Ennio Morricone at 6:30am in the Morning.

The Music came to a stop and the track on my Ipod finised and I stopped running and walked to the Gate of the Cemetery. In the evening I did some drawing of me in the Spa of Eusebius doing Shaman drumming therapy. I have also ordered some Paints felt-tips from Japan. The felt-tips make is Uni Posca and come in many different Colours. I have enrolled on a Art Illustration Course that starts on the 15th January 2014 at Wirral Met College and also enrolled on a learn to draw in Water-colours. I am looking forward to doing my Art Courses in January 2014 and I like the idea of becoming an Artist.

22nd November 2013

I was given a Red BMX bike by the Rampworx staff as I had come for an evening lesson on how to use a BMX bike in a Skatepark. I had come to Rampworx Skatepark in Liverpoool to try BMX biking going over Ramps and doing Jumps. My instructor for the evening showed me how to ride the BMX bike over ramps and I even did a few Jumps which I was made up with. During the evening the Instructor showed me the foam pit where I could have a go at trying tricks and crash into the foam square blocks that where in the pit. I decided to have ago at trying a trick on the BMX bike and then I found myself doing a trick in mid-air and then I crashed into the foam pit and because I have some weight on my body, I found myself at the bottom of the pit, which caused some amusement to people that where around the foam pit. This never put me off trying another trick and once again crashing into the foam pit. I would say that the square foam pit was the highlight of the evening and I really enjoyed BMX biking at Rampworx.

23rd November 2013

I took my place in the Queue for my Catapult Bungee jump with the UK Bungee Club. A Catapult Bungee Jump is a reverse Jump, where I will get shot 150 feet into the Air and plummet back down to Earth with the Bungee cord to stop me. Soon it was my turn to do the Catapult reverse Bungee Jump. The UK Bungee Club Staff put a safety harness around my waist and then I was asked whether I was ready to do this Catapult reverse Jump. I was ready to do this extreme Adventure and before I knew it, the instructor pulled a cord and I went hurtling through the Air at a great speed. Once I got to a good height I then started dropping to the Ground at a fast speed and my Adrenaline was going. At the end of the Catapult reverse Bungee Jump I had become very excited and very hyper-active. On the way home I called into the Entertainer Toy Shop to see if they had any Rubik 360 Puzzle sphere. I do like a good puzzle and I have been looking at the Rubik 360 puzzle sphere on the Internet.

24th November 2013

I arrived at the address in Bromborough and phoned the mobile number that the lady had given me. I rung the number and a lady answered the telephone and gave me directions to her house. I knocked on the house door that I was directed to and was greeted by a lovely Lady in her forties with Red Hair and wearing a royal Blue indian Saree. The Lady greeted me and she had a very Beautiful smile and she looked lovely in her indian Saree. The Lady showed me a room which she had prepared and there was a therapy Bed in the middle of the room covered with dark Red towels, also there was lit candles around the room and soft Sitar music playing in the Background.

I was asked to take my clothes off and leave them on the Chair provided. The Lady left the Room and I took off my clothes and lay on my side on the therapy table with the lower half of my body covered with the dark Red towel. What followed in the next 90 minutes was the most intense experience I have had so far. The experience was a Massage of my Prostate and was very relaxing and is called Tantra Therapy.

25th November 2013

I was at the Barber's this evening for another new experience. I had come to the Barber's for a Cut Throat Razor shave and I was slightly nervous about having this kind of shave. When I booked the experience, the Barber told me not to Shave for at least 3 days. In the end I haven't Shaved my face and neck for 5 days and I was starting to look a bit hairy and been in a Submarine for 3 months look.

The Barber was a Lady and she asked me to take a seat by the wash basin in a reclining Barber Chair. I took a seat in the reclining chair and then the Lady Barber put a towel over me and then started putting shaving cream on my face and neck. Then she picked up a Cut throat Razor and told me to relax as much as possible while she shaved my face with the cut throat razor. I relaxed as much as possible as the Lady Barber shaved my face and neck. I found the Shaving experience to be some-what eroctic in nature, as I sat there and let a Women shave me with a cut throat Razor. After the Shave the Lady Barber gave me a Scalp Massage.

26th November 2013

The Flare-gun went off and the Lifeboat was scrambled and then launched. The Crew took there positions on the Rigid Inflatable Lifeboat and once the lifeboat was on the water it made it's way to where the Emergency was. As the Lifeboat got nearer to the emergency scene which was a metal bouy about half a mile out to Sean from the New Brighton Shore-Line. The Lifeboat Crew could see a Dolphin tail in the Water and a Man with a dark brown ladies wig on and the lower half of his body covered in what looked like Fish Scales. The Lifeboat came along side me and asked if I was alright, I asked the Lifeboat Crew if they had ever come across a Mermaid before and the answer I was given was "No". The Lifeboat Crew helped me into the Lifeboat and put a Space Blanket around me and then the Lifeboat went back to the Shore at Speed and to my Surprise there was an Ambulance waiting for me. I was taken to Hospital with my Fishtail still attached to me and I was quite a sight when I arrived at the A&E department at the Wirral University Hospital, the Nurses fell in love me and one of the Nurses got me a Cuddly Toy Fish to take Home with me.

27th November 2013

I was given strict orders to stay on Dry Land today by the Hospital Staff as I didn't realise I had Hyperthermia. Mum and Dad was mad with me as what I did was very stupid and extremely dangerous. I spent the morning on the Dining room table playing with my Toy Knights. In the afternoon Dad took me to Bromborough and I went to get the Hex Bugs V2 Blackhole Habitat. Hex Bugs V2 are small Bugs that vibrate and can go upside down and can even climb. We got home for 3:30pm and then I made filtered Coffee for everyone. For Tea we had Cheeseburger and french fries and I had Heinz Tomatoe Ketchup. I also had seven sweet Pickles with small tomatoes and a side dish of Lettuce. Desert was a Walls Magnum ice-cream which was very nice. In the evening I played with my remote control 1:36 scale micro-T truggy which is really fast on the Landing and the little remote control Model is very good at going downstairs as well. I have a 1:10 scale Dune Buggy which has a brushed motor and I am going to upgrade the Model to a Brushless Motor.

28th November 2013

I had come to Shropshire to experience driving a Hovercraft and I was quite excited about this experience. I arrived at the Hovercraft Centre in Shropshire for about 10:30am with my Hovercraft experience booked for 11:00 am. I booked in for the experience at the reception desk and then the instructor showed me the Hovercraft I would be using. I was very impressed by the Hovercraft. The instructor climbed aboard the Hovercraft and then asked me to sit behind him and we then took the Hovercraft around the Course. The ride on the Hovercraft was a strange experience, it was like floating on a cushion of Air, which I think that how Hovercrafts work. All I know is that when I took the controls of the Hovercraft it never steered in the direction I wanted it too, and was very difficult to control, and as usual the instructor made it look easy. At the end of the Hovercraft experience the instructor gave me a Certificate saying I had experienced controlling a Hovercraft. I had enjoyed my Hovercraft experience and I found out that Hovercrafts are very hard to control. In New Brighton they have a Lifeboat Rescue Hovercraft for inshore use.

29th November 2013

I parked my Car in Wavertree Leisure Centre Car-park and then paid my money at the reception desk to go for a swim. I had come to Wavertree Leisure Centre as it has a 50 metre swimming pool and is the largest indoor Swimming Pool on Merseyside. I got changed and put my swimming trunks on and then made my way out of the Changing room and onto the Poolside. What greeted me when I got to the pool Side was a full size 50 metre Olympic Swimming Pool. I have only seen these size swimming Pools on the Television when watching the Common Wealth Games or the Olympic Games. The only other large swimming Pool I swim in is the Dock, which is basically a glorified Open Air Lido to swim in during the Summer Months. I swum a 100 lengths of the 50 metre Pool and each Length seemed to take ages to complete as I am use to swimming in a 25 metre indoor swimming Pool. After the swim I got a Coffee from the Cafe area and treated myself to a piece of Chocolate Cake. While drinking my Coffee I looked at a Guitar Website where Dad has told me that a Company make a effect pedal that makes a Guitar into a Indian Sitar, as I was thinking of ordering a Indian Sitar from India through the Auction Site Ebay.

30th November 2013

I had come to the fetish Club on the Wirral to once again become a Geisha. I did my make-up on the 3rd floor of the Club using a bathroom Mirror. I use a white paste make-up called Mehron White for the Geisha White make-up and I use Blue eye shadow and Red Lipstick which is very striking with the White make-up. I use a powder puff on my face and neck area so the make-up doesn't go onto the Kimono's. Once I had done my make-up I then put the Jupan on which is a under kimono and then tied a cord around my waist to pull the Jupan Kimono tight. Then I put the Main Kimono on that I had bought recently from Osaka, Japan. The main Kimono was Pink and White and looked good with the Multi coloured Jupan. I put the main Kimono on and then I wrapped an Obi belt around my waist and pulled the Obi belt tight so it became similar to wearing a Corset. The last item to put on in my Geisha Regalia was the Geisha Katsura Wig that I got from Japan and is a genuine Geisha Wig and is very heavy to wear. After putting on all the Geisha Regalia I made my way to the second floor and saw a Beautiful Geisha in the Mirror and I had now transformed into a Beautiful Butterfly.

1st December 2013

I have come to Blackpool with my Dad to see the Funny Girls Christmas Extravaganza Show. We took our seats in the Theatre for the Show to begin and then a very Sexy Blonde haired Women with a sexy Red Christmas Costume come on Stage. I love the Mariah Carey Music Video with Mariah Carey in the Sexy Red Christmas Costume singing "all I want for Christmas is you", it certainly fires my Button with this Great Music Video. The show started and it was a lot of Fun watching the women dancing and wearing Corsets and they looked very glamourous in all of the different costumes they put on. The show was very similar to the Burlesque Show that I went to see at the Floral Pavilion in New Brighton. I sat in the Theatre and watched the Women doing there Dances and I was slightly getting Hot flushes from watching these beautiful Women dancing. The show finished and we made our way back to the Car and realised that the Car had Iced up, so we used a small De-icer spray that Dad had with him and then we de-iced the Care and then made our way home, in the review Mirror I could see Blackpool Tower Lit up.

2nd December 2013

I tried as hard as I could to put the Ice Skates on and I eventually got the Ice Skates on and was ready to try Ice Skating at Deeside Ice Skating Ring. I tried to stand up and I found out very quickly that standing up on Ice Skates is very Hard. I made my way onto the Ice Skating ring and used the side Barriers to find my balance on the Ice. Myself like other people at the Ice Skating Ring was holding onto the side Rails and we dared not let go for the fear of falling onto the Ice. I found some courage and let go of the side rails and was rewarded with my Arms and Legs going in different directions and I fell hard on my bum onto the cold ice. When I fell on my Bum I really fell over with some force and it was definitely painful. So I decided to exit the Ice Skating Ring. I eventually managed to get off the Ice Ring and I took the Ice Skates off and went to the cafe to warm myself up. I can't say I enjoyed the experience of Ice Skating as you can find yourself being injured very quickly and I tried hard to balance but found even standing on the ice ring to be a mammoth Task.

3rd December 2013

I met up with 3 people who enjoy Urban Exploring and I made sure my Torch was working. We had come to explore Oil Complex in Birkenhead which has been abandoned for years. Urban exploring is where you explore around abandoned Building, and is quite an Adrenaline Rush. This was my first time doing Urban Exploring and I was looking forward to seeing inside the Oil Complex in Birkenhead. Soon i found myself climbing a metal Ladder that lead to Chemical tanks that we walked over. Then we climbed down another Ladder and made our way into a Open metal door and we found our way into a Warehouse filled with old Oil Drums and pieces of metal and rubbish laying on the floor of the Warehouse. We went through the Warehouse and then climbed another metal Ladder to a Chemical Storage tank that was about 50 feet high. After climbing the 50ft storage tank, we made our along a series of Storage tanks until we came across a Metal Ladder and made our way down the ladder and we came to a pumping station. In the distance we could see a torch coming towards us and we hid under a cover that was near the Pumping station, I enjoyed trying Urban Exploring and was quite a unique experience.

4th December 2013

Mum and Dad had taken me to Buffalo Jacks American Diner this evening. Buffalo Jacks Diner is located in Queens Square, Liverpool. I fell in Love with the American themed Diner with pictures of New York on the Wall. The American Diner had a resin statue of Elvis and also two resin statues of the Blues Brothers. We took our seats at one of the wooden tables and then looked at the Menu and there was a lot of choice on the Menu. I decided to go for a Cheeseburger served with Fries and a side dish of Salad. The waitress took our orders and then we got some drinks and waited for our meals to arrive. Our meals we ordered came and I couldn't believe the size of the Cheeseburger it was huge and took half the plate up. I served the Tomatoe ketchup and put some ketchup on my Cheeseburger and also some sauce for the fries. I enjoyed my meal at Buffalo Jacks in Liverpool and for desert I had Chocolate Ice Cream with hot Chocolate Fudge Cake. I enjoyed listening to the Rock N' Roll music from the Diner Juke Box and I even chose a track myself which was the Song "My Rocket 88". There is a American themed Diner at Cheshire Oaks in Ellesmereport for me to visit later in the Month.

5th December 2013

I had come to an evening of Snow fun at Chill factor, Trafford Park, Manchester. I started this Snow evening using a Snowscoot which is like a bmx bike on a Snowboard and I had a lot of fun using the Snowscoot. Next on my snow evening Adventure I went on the Avalanche ride, which is a inflatable Sphere where you are strapped inside a ball and then you roll down the Ski slope at Speed. After trying the Avalanche I tried extreme sledging where I used the main slope and sledged down the slope at a very good speed. I was getting slightly cold so I decided to get a Coffee and visit the Cafe and the shopping area of Chill factor. After having my Coffee I tried Airboarding which you lay on inflatable bodyboard and slide down a Snow Slope. Then once I finished playing on the Airboards I went on the Luge Ride. My final bit of fun for the evening was experiencing Tubing. Tubing is where you sit in the Centre of an inflatable ring and you get pushed down a small slope and tubing is quite a thrilling experience and I have enjoyed my evening at Chill Factor and I enjoyed all the different activities that was on offer at Chill Factor, I had a great time at Chill Factor.

6th December 2013

This evening I went to Starbuck's Coffee shop in New Brighton. The rain was coming down quite hard and it was very fine rain which would soak you to the Bone. I ordered myself a filtered Americano Coffee and sat down in a plush chair to drink my Coffee. I sat down and watched the rain through the Window. For all my Adventures that I do, I am a very Lonely person and don't have any friends other then the people I swim with. I have never been on a Night out or been to a Night Club or enjoyed going to Kebab house in the earlier hours of the morning. I can't read people signals or understand what they say and I would end up being hurt. That is not going to stop me from attending a Medieval Christmas Banquet at Ruthin Castle tomorrow evening as I am looking forward to this Adventure. I kept looking at the Rain through the Window and I decided I would visit Father Christmas in Lapland and go on a Sleigh Ride pulled by a Reindeer. When I got home I done some research on Day trips to Lapland from John Lennon Airport, Liverpool. I chose a Day Trip to Lapland to see Father Christmas on the 20th December 2013 and I would fly from John Lennon Airport to Lapland. This would be the first time I have flown in a commercial Airplane.

7th December 2013

I took my place with all the other people that had come to this Medieval Banquet at Ruthin Castle, North Wales. Once we where all seated the maids served the Food and Beer, which was a lot of different meats and the Beer was a nice Ruby Ale which I enjoyed drinking. The food spread for the Medieval Banquet was very impressive. The large Christmas Tree in the Banquet Hall made the Banquet a very festive scene. There was also entertainment with a Juggler and fire eater. At 11pm I retired to my Hotel Bedroom in Ruthin castle to sleep for the Night. The room I stopped in had stone walls and was Tudor period 4 poster Bed with a desk and a chair to one side of the Bed. During the Night I woke up and I felt the room was very cold and then I noticed a dark shadow at the end of the Bed and my Blood went cold as I sat there in Bed looking at this Dark Shadow. After a couple of minutes the Dark Shadow disappeared through one of the stone Wall. I spent the rest of the night hiding under the Blankets of the Bed as the temperature of the room never altered. I got back to sleep about 4am not knowing what the Dark Shadow was that had entered the Room.

8th December 2013

After a Night seeing what I thought was a ghost in my Hotel Bedroom, I decided to walk around the Grounds of the Castle. The Castle grounds was very magical and it was like being in the Winter Wonderland of Narnia. I came across a frozen Pond and I looked at my reflection in the Ice. By the Pond I found a log to sit on and watched the Sun make different Colours within the Ice that covered the Pond. My Love of Colours comes from my Heart and I Love drawing and Creative Imagination.

At 2pm I made my way back home to Wallasey and found that my Parcel had arrived from Japan. The Parcel was the Felt-tip coloured Pens that I ordered and the Coloured Pens make Uni-Posca, some of the best coloured felt-tips Pens on the Market. I did another drawing of me at the Spa of Eusebius doing Hypoxi therapy, which is you wear a suit similar to a drysuit with socket cups where hoses attaches to the suit and then the hoses are connected to a Vacuum suction and you definitely feel the suction in the suit and is quite a strange experience. I had Hypoxi treatment in my Adventures from February 2010 to May 2013.

9th December 2013

I was all wired up with electrodes on my forehead and had ECG electrodes attached to the upper part of my body and I had a Blood Pressure monitor on my left upper arm. The electrodes attached to my head was for EEG that measures Brain activity. I had come to Liverpool University to take part in some research and was having an EEG study in the morning and this afternoon I was at (MARIARC) magnetic resonance and Image Research Centre. I went to the MARIARC centre in Liverpool to do the second part of the research which was an MRI scan of my Brain. I signed in at the reception desk and then one of the Centre Nurses took me to a changing cubicle and I changed into a hospital gown and then the Nurse took me to the MRI machine and I was asked to lay on the MRI bed and a strap went across my forehead so I couldn't move my head, I was given a squeeze bulb in my right hand, to squeeze if I panicked in the MRI tunnel. The MRI scan was very loud and very noisy and I was made up with the Ear plugs that where given to me before I went into the MRI Machine.

10th December 2013

I took my seat in the Liverpool Philharmonic hall and waited for the Concert to start. I had come to listen to the Bootleg Beatles which is a tribute Band to the Beatles Pop Group. I had heard a lot about this tribute Band and I was told that they were very good and where the best Beatles tribute Band Around. The Bootleg Beatles came on Stage and where in the Beatles earlier 1960's outfits. When the Bootleg Beatles started playing I actually thought they where the real Beatles as they where that good. The first part of the Bootleg Beatles was the music from the earlier Years of the Beatle Anthology. At the half time interval I had a Shandy in the Lounge and Bar area on the 1st floor of the Liverpool Philharmonic. I enjoyed drinking my Shandy and it was soon time for the second part of the Bootleg Beatles Concert. The second part of the Concert was from Sgt Pepper's Album to there last Album 'Let it Be'. The Bootleg Beatles Sgt Pepper costumes where very good and very well made. When the concert finished I found myself shouting for them to play more Beatle Songs and the Bootleg Beatles came back on stage and played two more songs.

11th December 2013

I had come to Hoylake Community Centre to experience spiritual Meditation in Buddhism. I have always wanted to try Meditation and I wondered what it was going to be like. The Meditation Tutor was a Women and her name was Jayne. Jayne put new comers at ease, going through the techniques of slow breathing and the steps to complete relaxation and to open your mind to Spiritual awakening. The technique of Meditation is not as easy as it looks, as you have to empty your mind completely and concentrate on your breathing. During the Meditation class I was very relaxed and concentrating on my breathing, although I never got to the state of Nirvana. I did manage to go into a trance like state of Blissfulness. At the end of Meditation class our tutor Jayne gave everyone a Flower and to let Sunshine into our Hearts and too see the Colour of the Rainbow. I had enjoyed my Meditation experience and I learnt a lot of things on how to relax and how to control my breathing. After the Meditation class I listened to Indian Sitar Music on the way Home and I was feeling the Vibe of the Flower Power Generation at last.

12th December 2013

This evening I had come to Spire Hospital at Murrayfields on the Wirral for a Medical Assessment that I had brought from Living Social Voucher website. I reported to the Hospital reception desk and then took a seat in the waiting area. A Nurse came to greet me and she had a very warmful Smile to her. I followed the Nurse to the Exam room and was given a thorough Medical. My Blood Pressure was taken and Blood Samples, as well as my height and weight. Also as part of my Medical at the Spire Hospital I had and ECG Heart trace done and also a Bone Dexa scan, which I didn't really fully understand the Dexa Scan. The Dexa Scanner was something you would see in a science fiction film it was a impressive piece of Equipment. The ECG Heart trace was done and I was given a copy of the Heart trace which will come in useful when I do the Ice Mile Swim later in the Month at West Kirby Marine Lake. My Dexa scan came back normal which was very positive. After the Medical I went home and looked at purchasing the HDX Ravish Sitar effect Machine for Electric Guitar, I have seen lots of good reviews for the Ravish Sitar on the internet and I have watched people using the Ravish effect machine on the Youtube Video Site.

13th December 2013

I relaxed on my side on the therapy Bed as the Therapist put a Lit Candle in my Ear. I have come to Hopi Ear Candle wax remover therapy and I was slightly nervous about having someone stick candle in my Ear. When i'm at Home I use the Eye of a sewing Needle to get Wax out of my Ears and I go into a Trance like state when I am removing my Ear wax from my Ears. This evening was no different as soon as the therapist put the Candle in my Ears, I could feel the Wax in my ear being sucked out and I went into a trance like state with my eyes fixed while Hopi Candling therapy was performed on me. After the Hopi Ear Candling Session the Therapist gave my Ears a delightful massage which sent my senses wild with Pure Joy. After the Ear massage I was given a couple of minutes to relax and gently sit up and then find my balance. I had enjoyed my Hopi Ear Therapy and Ear massage and the therapist didn't recommend sticking a Sewing Needle down my ears and I could harm or pierce my Eardrum. It was then I realised I wanted to have my Belly Button pierced as I go all Giddy when I tickle my Belly Button.

14th December 2013

I lay in the Floatation tank virtually weightlessness and I concentrated on my breathing that I had learnt from Jayne the tutor at the Meditation class in Hoylake Community centre. I arrived at Cherry Floatation tank centre at 10am and was greeted by the Centre staff as I walked through the door. I was shown the Floatation tank and then I undressed in a changing cubicle, I had a choice whether to Float naked or with a swim costume. I decided to go for the full experience and to float in the Floatation tank naked. I made my way to the Floatation tank and the Pool was about 2 feet deep and then I sat down in the Water and then I hesitated for a moment as this quite strange for what I was going to do is float on water which is quite an unnatural thing to do. After a couple of minutes I lay in the floatation tank and let myself float on the Water. It was a strange feeling and very enjoyable at the same time. Once I was floating the staff came on the speaker and asked if I was alright and then I floated in the calmness and Bliss of the Floatation Tank.

15th December 2013

The Glider took a sharp bank to the left and I could see the Mountains of the Lake District. Through the cockpit of the Glider I took in the Beautiful views of the lush scenery that was on offer. The Pilot during my Gliding experience even took the Glider upside down and it was a lot of Fun soaring through the Sky in a Glider. The Capsule over the Glider's cockpit was very much like a Bubble which I could see out of. I was taken in the views when suddenly the Pilot put the Glider into a Nose dive and the Glider started hurtling down to Earth. Then the Pilot put the steering stick backwards and the Glider went upside down again and did a complete loop the loop above the skies of the Lake District. Soon it was time for us to go back to the airfield and then the Pilot landed the Glider and I was back down on Earth again. I thanked the Pilot for taking me flying in a Glider and it was given a Certificate by the Gliding School to say that I had flown in a Glider in the Lake District in Lancashire.

16th December 2013

Me and Mum had come to Liverpool City Centre to do some Christmas shopping and to look around the World Christmas Market and sample different foods from around the World. There was a stall from Peru that sold bobble hats and Wool hoodies that where Multi-coloured and also sold Shaman Drums. We tried a Spicy German Sausage in a Barn Cake which we really enjoyed eating and then we looked around Liverpool One, Liverpool Main shopping Centre. We went into John Lewis Department Store and got my first look at a Sony Playstation 4 which I thought looked very sleek and Modern. I also went into the Lego Shop and looked at a Lego Set which is a Volkswagon Campervan. After looking around Liverpool One shopping Centre we went to Weatherspoon Pub for a Pub Lunch and I had Gammon Steak with a slice of Pinapple, egg and Chips, mixed with a fusion of Tomatoe Ketch-up. Later in the Afternoon Mum was getting Cold so we got the Train Home. The Train platform was quite busy with other shoppers that had done there Christmas Shopping. Once we got Home I made Mum and Dad a nice cup of Yorkshire Tea.

17th December 2013

Me and Mum had come to Ed's Diner at Cheshire Oaks at the Outlet Village in Ellesmereport. This is my second American themed Diner that I had gone too this Year. We took our seats in one of the Booths and there was even a small juke Box on the Table and I put a coin into the Juke Box and chose a Rock and Roll Song. The waitress was dressed in a 1950's American diner waitress outfit and she took our orders for the Food. Once again I chose a Cheeseburger with American Fries and Tomatoe Ketchup. I really enjoyed eating at Ed's Diner and the food was very good. After eating we had a look around Cheshire Oaks outlet Village and I went into my Favourite Clothes Shops and got myself some New Clothes. The Tall Christmas Tree shone very bright and looked very Magical and I Cheshire Oaks Christmas Tree is the tallest Christmas tree in Europe. In the late afternoon Me and Mum had a coffe in Costa Coffee and then we had a look around Marks and Spencers Outlet Shop and then we headed for Home. In the evening I watched a Documentary about a Diver that went looking for Treasure in the Sea of Florida Quays, United states of America.

18th December 2013

The Driving Instructor showed me the Controls and how to drive a Lamboghini Gallardo LP 550-2.
I had come to Donnington Park Race track for a Super Car thrill Day, which you can buy on the Internet. The Super Car that I had chosen to drive was a Lamborghini Gallardo in superb Orange. Once I learnt the controls I was ready to drive the Lamboghini around Donnington Park Race track. The acceleration and aggressiveness of the Super Car was amazing and the Sheer speed of the Car meant I found my whole Body tightening around the steering Wheel and my face felt as if it was pushing inwards. I loved driving the Lamboghini Gallardo around Donnington Park race track and I just wanted to keep driving this Car. But sadly after the set laps of my Super Car thrill drive I had to go back to the Garage and give the Lamboghini Gallardo back. I had gone past 100 mph + with the Lamboghini and when I got back into my Car I had to realise that my Honda Jazz 1.4 EX is not a Lamboghini Gallardo and I soon settled down to everyday driving, but I still want a Lamboghini Gallardo LP 550-2.

19th December 2013

I arrived at Liverpool City Centre for 9:30am and I wasn't in Liverpool to do Christmas Shopping, I had come on an invitation to climb a Sky Crane. I had wrote to a company a couple of months ago to ask could I climb a Sky Crane and to my surprise I got an invitation to climb a Sky Crane with two members of the Company Staff. I met up with the Two Men that where going to climb the Sky Crane with me and they first gave me a safety talk and then we proceeded to the Sky Crane. Before we climbed the Sky Crane I was given a safety Harness and safety Equipment to wear. Once the two men where happy with my safety equipment, we then started climbing the Sky crane. The Climb to the top of the Sky Crane was a series of ladders and I enjoyed climbing the Sky crane and we soon found ourselfs at the Top of the Sky Crane and then we made our way to the Crane cockpit where the Crane driver sits. I was allowed to sit in the Crane Drivers seat and I am glad I don't have a fear of heights as the cockpit had a glass floor and was a long way down. Soon it was time to climb down from the Sky crane and put my feet on hard concrete.

20th December 2013

I got off the Airplane at Ivalo Airport and was greeted by Elf's who were offering Hot soup in a Log Cabin. After I ate the Soup a Lady Elf helped me get into Thermal Clothing and one piece thermal suit for my Lapland Adventure Day. Once I put my thermal clothing on and woolly Hat I joined the queue to board the Coach for the 25 minute Journey to the start of my Lapland experience. The Coach stopped in a Car Park and then an Elf came on Board the Coach and asked everyone to follow her to a Wooden log cabin. I followed the elf to the Log Cabin and then after a Hot Drink I made my way to the Sleigh experience. The Sleigh experience was going for a ride in a Sleigh pulled by Two Reindeer and was amazing experience. At the end of the Sleigh Ride the driver of the Sleigh stopped the Sleigh outside of a Wooden Log cabin and I went inside the Log Cabin and there He was sitting by the Fire place in arm chair keeping himself Warm. On the flight Home I saw Aurora Borealis, the Northern lights and watched the Lights display. I have had a very Magical Day today and I have enjoyed my Lapland Winter Adventure Day to the Artic.

21st December 2013

I was getting very hyper-active today after my visit to Lapland and I had booked a Hot Mud wrap at the Local Salon to calm me down. The Therapist covered my whole Body in Hot Mud and then wrapped me up in what looked like tinfoil and then a plastic Sheet was covered over and then I was cocooned in Mud. The therapist also put hot towels over me to keep me warm and also put a cover over my eyes and gave me a deep relaxing scalp massage. I told the therapist all about yesterday Adventure in Lapland and the Therapist understood why I had booked a hot mud body wrap as I needed unwind from yesterday excitement. I was also excited about the Ice Mile swim that I was doing tomorrow at West Kirby Marine Lake, but for now I lay back and let the hot mud take away all my aches and pains that my body has produced throughout the Year. I have put my Body through a lot of punishment this Year as well as depression that covered me to have an overdose which my Body has never really recovered from. On the outside I look the same person to everyone, but on the inside I am in a lot of Pain and my head always hurt a great deal.

22nd December 2013

The Water' temperature was taken and West Kirby Marine Lake was 4 oC degrees or below for the Rules of the Ice Mile Swim is that the Water temperature must be below 50C degrees. I had a Rigid inflatable for safety cover and a Canoeist that would help me by guiding me down the Lake. Also in attendance was a Research Doctor from John Moores University which was great as it was a Lady Doctor who was going to monitor my Vitals for the Ice Mile Swim. I was doing the Ice Mile with no Wetsuit and I was hoping I wouldn't swim into any sharp Ice while swimming in the Lake. As soon as the safety crew was ready, I was given the Green light to enter the Water to start my Ice Mile Swim. The water was very cold and my face went Numb as I put my face in the Water. I started swimming down the Lake to the other end of the lake and back again for it to be an Ice Mile. I concentrated on my breathing that I had learnt in the meditation class and I fixed my mind on my drawing that I enjoy creating. I soon found myself at the other end of the Lake and I turned around and swam back to the start, I completed my Ice Mile swim and then I was wrapped up in Space Blankets and the Lady Doctor took my Vitals.

23rd December 2013

I helped Dad put the Christmas Lights up in Back Garden and it took us a good while to put all the lights up. After putting all the Lights up, Mum came outside to switch all the Lights on and soon the whole of the Back Garden was Lit up with different coloured Lights and the Back Garden looked very Beautiful. After switching on the Lights I decided to have a cup of filtered Coffee and sit in the back Garden and look at the Illuminations that decorated the Back Garden. The cold stillness of the Night Air filled my Lungs as I sat there and reflected on all my Adventures that I had done over the last 4 years and all the People I have encountered along the way. Soon I was getting cold from sitting outside and I decided to go inside. Once I got inside I decided to put all my Hotwheel Cars on the Dining room table and assemble the Hotwheel track in the Dining Room which had two loops so the Hotwheel cars could go upside down. I played with the Hotwheel Track for a good couple of hours and I have Hotwheel Cars that change colour if you soak them with Water. Soon it was time to have a Shower and go to bed.

24th December 2013

I wrapped Christmas Presents in my Bedroom while listening to Music and I was definitely in the Festive Spirit. This afternoon I had watched the Film Santa Claus and I experienced a Magical day in Lapland. I wrapped the Christmas presents and then I went downstairs to find Mum had poured some Hot Mulled Wine into little Glasses for the Family to drink. I took a Glass of hot Mulled wine and I felt all warm and I felt all Dandy and Bubbly after drinking the mulled wine. In the evening I watched some more Christmas films and before I went to Bed I put some Jam Tarts and mulled Wine outside for Father Christmas so he doesn't get hungry when he would come late into the Christmas Night. Once I had my Supper I snuggled up in Bed with Herbert my Cuddly Toy Dinosaur and watched a late Night movie, in the hope I would see Father Christmas Sleigh going through the Night Sky. However I soon fell a sleep as the Medication I take at night helps me relax and I fell a sleep. So I don't end up wandering around the House in the earlier Hours of the morning, looking for Father Christmas.

25th December 2013

Mum woke Me and Lee up and told us that a cooked Breakfast would be ready on the Dining room table at 9:30am. The cooked Breakfast was nice and the fresh orange juice woke me up and I took my morning medicine. After the cooked Breakfast me and my Brother Lee washed all the dishes that had been used to make the Cooked Breakfast, while Mum and Dad went to sit down in the Living Room. Once the dishes where done me and Lee went into the Living Room where there was Christmas Presents put on the Settee for Me and Lee. I got a Longboard Skateboard for Christmas as well as a Kahuna Paddle Stick, so I could go Paddle Boarding in New Brighton. I got some Computer Games for Christmas from my Brother Lee and I got lots of Sweets and goodies as well.

We had Christmas Dinner at 3pm and I poured the Sparkling Wine for everyone. I got a Toy Comb in my Cracker and Lee got a small Rubik Cube. Later in the Evening we had a Buffet with cold meats and desert was Christmas Cake that Mum had made earlier in the Month. After the Buffet I watched Man of Steel (Superman) Movie and I ate Salt and Vinegar Kettle Crisps in my Bedroom.

26th December 2013

I took my position on the Wooden Jetty with the Nine other swimmers that where going to swim the 400 metres swim to the slipway of Salthouse Dock, Liverpool. The Water Temperature of the Dock was 0c degrees and was very cold. Then the whistle was blown and the ten of us that where swimming the Dock jumped into the freezing cold water and began to swim the Length of the Dock back down to the slipway. As like the ice Mile Swim, my face went numb as it went into the Water and I could feel the cold around my eye sockets. I wasted no time when I got into the Water as I started swimming towards the slipway as fast as I could. I soon reached the slipway and got out of the Water and then I made my way to my swim Bag with Dry Clothes and a towel. I got changed and got myself warm by drinking Hot Chocolate and putting my warm Ski coat on. After the Boxing Day swim I went home and we had a Family dinner which was a Roast Beef and then I watched some more Christmas Movies and looked at my new Remote Control Car which is HPI Sprint Flux 2 and the Body Shell was Chevelot Camaro 2010.

27th December 2013

This morning I attended a Christmas Lecture at Liverpool University and the Lecture was about the exploration of Space and the Race to the Moon. I took my seat in the Lecture Hall and waited for the Lecture on Space to Start. The Lecture was very good and it started by looking at the earlier space flights by Nasa and Russia before moving onto the Race to the Moon and the Saturn 5 Rockets. The last part of the Lecture was about the Space Shuttle and the International Space Station and understanding the Dangers of the exploration of Space. I sat in the lecture hall day dreaming about going into space and seeing the Earth from the Moon. After the lecture at Liverpool University I made my way through the concrete Jungle to Limestreet Train and the train platform to take me back to Wallasey. In the afternoon I played on my Sony Playstation 3 and played Ratchet and Clank into the Nexus which is a kind of Cartoon Cat with a Robot called Clank strapped to it's back and defends the Galaxy from evil villians. Soon it was evening and I looked out of my Bedroom Window at the street light that always been there lighting up the Avenue every night.

28th December 2013

I went to New Brighton with Dad this morning and took my Paddle-board and stick as well as the Remote control Cars, motorbikes and Boats. I tried Paddle-boarding for my first time on New Brighton Promenade and was difficult to get the hang of it the first time around. I eventually got the hang of paddle-boarding and I fell in Love with Longboard and Kahuna Stick. After a good 40 minutes of Paddle-boarding I then played with my remote control Speed Boat on the Model Boating Lake which was a lot of fun. Then after I played with my model Boat we went to the playing fields and Dad played with his Remote Control Motorbikes, which are dirt bikes and are really cool to watch. While Dad was playing with his r/c motorbikes, I got my r/c Buggy out the back of the Car and played with r/c Car on the Playing Field. Then once I had finished playing with the r/c Car I went over to the Sea Wall and looked out into Liverpool Bay. While standing at the Sea Wall I could hear the wind swirling around me and strange noises that whispered the Sirens of the Sea. I must of gone into a daze as I heard Dad calling out my name and then I went back onto the playing field and Dad let me play with the r/c motorbikes. When we got home I cleaned all the mud and Grass off the r/c models and Mum made Me and Dad had a filtered Coffee which I enjoyed drinking.

29th December 2013

I see the World through a Kaleidoscope, swirling around with many different coloured patterns to look at, my Adventures have been through the Glass of the Sovereign eye. To try and explain my 4 Year Journey is very difficult for me, as I am now trying to understand my Life that was suppose to end in May 2013 and it is now December 2013. The Great 3 Year Adventure was to end on the Shore on New Brighton Beach with me taking an overdose and swimming out into Liverpool Bay to become a Beautiful Fish. This never happened and I am slightly annoyed over this, as I love doing everything in detail down to the last measurement. I sat in the Dining room and watched the birds feeding from the bird feeders from the patio window. Lunch was Turkey sandwiches as you might guess the Turkey was very big that we had on Christmas Day and since then we have been eating Turkey Sandwiches and Turkey with Chips and so on. After dinner I watched Jules Verne 20 thousand Leagues under the Sea, which is a Great film to watch. Later in the evening I listened to Rock Music in my Bedroom and I have a set of drum sticks which I bang on my Bed and pretend the Bed is a set of Drums and usually end up being told off because of the noise drum sticks make through the floor boards as Mum and Dad can hear me from Downstairs.

30th December 2013

I struck a G Chord on my Danelectro Wild Thing Guitar as I was trying out my New HDX Ravish Sitar effect machine that make your Guitar sound like a Sitar. I was amazed by the Eastern sounds that this effect machine was creating. I played the Beatles 'Here comes the Sun' with Ravish Sitar effect machine and the results was a beautiful rich sound. I am glad I got this effect machine as I can sit on my Bed and play a Sitar without having to go to India to buy a Sitar, which would be very costly. I sat for hours on my Bed trying out different combinations that the Ravish sitar effect machine had to offer. I fell in Love with a couple of Combinations that I created with Ravish Sitar and one sound had a real echo to it. After playing my Guitar I went to the dining Room and did the last drawing for the Return to the Spa of Eusebius, which is me playing a Sitar in front of Arched Wooden Door and below me in a sunken room was a Egyptian Coffin with the Word Eusebius next to the Egyptian Coffin. I finished the Drawing and completed the Return Journey to the Great Spa of Aurora. After completing the Drawing I ran myself a nice Hot bath and then had a Pint of Wychwood Goliath Ruby Ale and a packet of Pickled onion Monster Munch.

31st December 2013

The Clock was fast approaching Midnight and I joyed the Family in the Living Room to bring in the New Year and watch Big Ben on the Television. Midnight arrived and the New Year Started and I had a slight tear in my Eye. I had a lot of things I am going to do in January 2014, I am going on a Winter Balloon Flight over the Cheshire plains on the 11th January 2014. I start my Art courses on the 15th January 2014 learning how to do Graphics and illustrations and the week later learning how to paint in Water-colours. In February I am going to see the Japanese Kodo drummers at the Liverpool Philharmonic Hall, Godzilla comes to the Cinema in May this Year. I want to ride the New rollercoaster at Alton Towers called Smiler and I would like to experience a European waterslide Park in Tenerife and have a Sailing Holiday on a Racing Yacht. After bringing the New Year in we gathered around the television and watched the Firework display which took place on the London Eye which is over-sized fairground Wheel. When the Firework display finished on the television I went back to my Bedroom and took my Medicine and went to Bed. It was now January 2014 and I was looking forward to New Adventures and my New Adventure Journal.

1st January 2014

I made my way along the Country Roads of North Wales, my destination was the Horse Shoe Pass with the Town of Llangollen at the bottom of the Valley. At the Top of the Horse Shoe Pass there is a Cafe where I got myself a nice hot bowl of Soup to warm the cockles of my Heart. Once I had eaten my soup I made my way to the Quarry of the Blue Lagoon.

I have come to the Quarry of the Blue Lagoon at the Horse Shoe Pass in North Wales, I made my way to the steepest Point of the Quarry walls which was roughly 100ft and prepared myself for what I was about to do. I had told everyone I was going to do a New Year Day swim in Manchester, but I wanted to something with a bit Adrenaline rush to start 2014 with a Giant leap. I took my clothes off and I had my swim short on underneath my Jeans, I left a my t-shirt on which is my favourite t-shirt that I like wearing. I had brought a pair of wetsuit socks that I put on as the slate on the

Ground was very cold on my Feet. I was now ready for the 100ft jump in the Ice cold Quarry, I made my way to the edge of the sheer drop and looked down at the Ice Cold Water that awaited me. I then paused for a moment and then jumped, I found myself hurtling towards the water and within a few seconds I hit the water. I went under the Ice cold Water and the Pure cold water turned into Darkness.

Epilogue
The Boat House by the Blue Lake

The Sun shone through the Window of my Art studio as I sat there drawing my next Painting. Out of the Window I could see the Beautiful Blue Lake that I swim in every Morning and evening before the Sunsets. My Art Studio was on the 1st floor of this Wooden Boat-house and downstairs was my Bedroom and a beautiful kitchen. Through a set of doors on the ground floor next to my Bedroom was a covered mooring for a Boat with a ladder that went into the Water. There was always plenty of food in the kitchen and had all my favourite foods in the fridge. I took in the view from my Art Studio of the Blue Lake and the last thing I remember was jumping into freezing cold water from 100ft at the Quarry of the Blue Lagoon on a cold January morning and then found myself sitting on a chair in Art Studio with a Beautiful warm Lake to swim in. Time stood still for me at the Boat-house, no one ever came and the Kitchen was always full of my favourite food. I swim in the evening and watch the Sun go down and there is never anyone with me to watch this Beautiful Sunset. The Night Sky is truly amazing, I watch different Planets and Moon circling one another, then after watching the Night Sky I go to my Bedroom and go to Bed. I wake up in my Bedroom at the Boat-house hoping someone will be here for me, but nobody comes and I go about my daily routine of a morning swim, breakfast which is a Bacon toastie and filtered Coffee and then I draw all day in my Art Studio on the first Floor. I Spend my Days at the Boat-house on my own and I draw and Paint in my Art Studio and watch the Sunrise and the Beautiful Sunset.

The Return to the Great Spa of Aurora
Written and drawn by Nicholas Robinson

The Glass Mirror Doorway to the Spa of Aurora

I put my Wizard Robe on in my Bedroom and put my Tudor Bonnet hat on my head and I then prepared myself for the New Journey to the Great Spa of Aurora. Once I had my wizard attire on, I made my way to the Bathroom where there was a Glass Mirror on the Wall by the side of the Bath.

I looked at the Mirrored wall in the Bathroom and I saw a wooden causeway in front of me and a set of two sandstone doors that led into an Entrance to the Spa of Aurora. I climbed over the white bath and walked through the Mirrored wall into the Garden of Aurora. I stood on the wooden Jetty and saw a beautiful Blue Sea and lots of Planets and Stars. I looked back and saw the Bathroom and the World of Black and White. I walked through the sandstone doors and noticed a painting on the wall and the name of Eusebius underneath the Painting. There was also three number Two in the Painting, there meaning was unclear to me. Below the Painting there was a metal bench which I sat on and then the sandstone Doors closed behind me.

Glass Mirror Entrance to the Great Spa of Aurora

Flower Slide to Spa of Aurora Reception

I sat on the metal bench and watched the Two sandstone Doors close behind me. In front of me was a Corridor and at the end of the Corridor was a Wooden Slide that lead into a Room with Yellow Coloured walls and beautiful coloured flowers and the room had a yellow stone floor.

There was a flower display dangling from the ceiling of this room. I decided to call this room the Flower Slide Room of the Great Spa of Aurora. To the left of the slide was a set of sandstone steps leading to the Spa Reception. I decided to slide down the Wooden Slide and then I made my way up the sandstone steps to the Spa Reception where I was greeted by one of the Nurses from the Great Spa of Aurora. The nurse introduced herself and the Nurses was Susan. I was asked to take a seat on the Blue Wooden bench. I was very excited about being back in the Great Spa of Aurora. I sat there and wondered what treatments I would be having at the Spa of Aurora. I had enjoyed the treatments that was done to me when I last came to the Spa of Aurora. When I first visited the Spa of Aurora I had a Medical from one of the Spa of Aurora Doctors and I wondered if I would be having a Medical again.

Flower Slide to the Spa of Aurora Reception

MRI Scan and Medical Assessment Suite

I took a seat on the Blue Wooden bench in the Reception area and then Susan left the reception desk and went down a corridor and then the Nurse went through a Door. After sitting on the Blue wooden bench for about 10 minutes I was starting to get hyper-active. Then another Nurse came out of the Door down the corridor and walked towards the Blue bench that I was sitting on. The Nurse introduced herself as Nurse Patterson and would I kindly follow the Nurse for an MRI scan of my Body. I followed the Nurse down the corridor to the MRI suite where there was a large machine with a round tube in the middle of the MRI scanner. The instructed me to go to the Changing cubicle next to the MRI scanner and put a Hospital Gown on. I did as instructed and I put on the nylon hospital gown and then tied the string in the middle of the Gown.

Once I put the hospital gown on I then went back to Nurse Patterson and the MRI scanner. Nurse Patterson asked me to lay down on the MRI scanner Bed and then once I had layered down on the MRI scanner bed the Nurse attached two plastic bars to my head and secured the bars to the bed which restrained my head. I now found that I couldn't move my head whilst I was in the MRI scanner.

Then the Nurse took two Broad straps and strapped my waist down and my lower legs to the MRI bed. The Nurse that the straps were put in place so I didn't move while I was in MRI Scanner.
The Nurse then put a squeeze bulb in my right hand and told me that if I panicked at any stage during the scan all I would have to do is squeeze the Bulb and I would be taken out of the Machine. Once the Nurse felt I was secure, the Nurse then made her way to the control room to operate the MRI Scanner. After a couple of minutes the MRI bed started to move into the MRI scanner Tunnel.

Then once I was comfortable the MRI Scanner began it's process of scanning my whole body. The MRI scanner was very noisy and it felt as if I had been in the scanner for a long while. Once the MRI scan of my Body was completed I was then taken out of the tunnel and then the Nurse told me to rest for a few minutes and then the Nurse unstrapped me from the MRI Scanner Bed and released the head restraints as well. The Nurse asked me to sit up and then stand up next to the MRI scanner bed. Once I was standing next to the MRI bed the Nurse asked if I could follow her to the medical Assessment Suite where Doctor Sandlove is waiting to see me about the results of the MRI Body Scan. I followed Nurse Patterson down a series of corridors and then we entered the Medical Assessment Suite. I gasped for breathe when I saw what was in front of me!

In front of me was a Metal chair with Blue restraints to restrain someone in which case I presumed that person would be me. The Nurse saw I was getting nervous and she told me to relax as the restraints are for me to let my Body relax. The Nurses guided me into the Metal chair and then secured all the restraining straps, Arms and legs and upper Body. The Nurse then put an extraction Collar around my neck and then I found I couldn't move my Neck at all. After putting the neck brace around my neck the Nurse then proceeded to restrain my head against high back rest of the metal chair.

I now found myself restrained to a metal chair in Medical Assessment suite. I used my eyes to have a look around the room which was the only thing on my body I could move as the Nurse had been very professional in securing me to the metal chair. In the room there was a lot of monitors and computers and a large LCD screen which I assumed to put MRI body scan on. In front of me was a grey chair and a Blue desk with a computer on the right hand corner of the desk. Suddenly after I looked around the room the Nurse started putting sticky pads on my chest. I knew this meant that I would be wired up to an ECG machine and they were going to listen to my Heart rhythm. After the Nurse connected me to the ECG machine. She then took 4 vials of Blood samples and I have to say the nurse was very good as it was only a sharp scratch when the Nurse put the Needle into my Arm to get the Blood Samples. Once the Nurse had the Blood samples the Doctor arrived and then sat at the Blue desk in front of me. The Doctor then greeted me and told me that her name was Doctor Claire Sandlove.

Doctor Sandlove after greeting me then looked at my MRI Body scan and then the Doctor took some notes down on a piece of Paper. After consulting the MRI scan and looking at the Medical Monitors, the Doctor was then ready to talk about my Treatments. The Doctor told me that I would be having Intensive Relaxation Treatment and that I needed to rest my Body for total relaxation.

The Doctor told me that I would be going into totally relaxed state and the treatment closely resembled in Intensive care Unit that you would find in a Hospital. I was then told after the Intensive Relaxation Treatment I would do other Therapies at the Spa of Eusebius another part of the Spa of Aurora I had not visited yet. Then after the Doctor completed her assessment, she then left the room and the Doctor wished me a lovely stay at the Great Spa of Aurora.

After the Doctor left the room the Nurse then came over to me and released the restraining straps that held me to the metal Chair. I was then asked to follow the Nurse to the Preparation Room. Before we left the Medical Assessment Suite the Nurse gave me a Pink Robe and a red tied cord to tie around the Pink Robe at the Waist.

Nicholas in Medical Assessment Suite, Great Spa of Aurora

Preparation Room for Intensive Relaxation

I followed Nurse Patterson to the Preparation room and on the way to the Preparation room the Nurse saw I was getting very Nervous about what the Doctor had told me about Intensive Relaxation Treatment. I thought to myself that I never had this therapy or treatment the last time I was at the Spa of Aurora. The Nurse saw that I was getting nervous and she told me to relax and the Nurse told me that this treatment is very relaxing for the Body and would let my Body have a lot of rest. I decided I would go with the flow and try the Intensive Relaxation Treatment at the Spa of Aurora. We entered the intensive Relaxation Preparation room and in front of me was a Hospital Gurney in the middle of the Room with wheels on the Gurney. Around the room there was trays with lots of Medical Equipment on them and there was different types of Medical equipment with lots of monitors attached to the Medical Equipment. After looking at the medical equipment I noticed I.V poles in the corner of the Preparation room and I assumed that the

I.V poles and the Drips attached was going to be put in arms at some point.

Nurse Patterson realised I was looking at all the medical Equipment and she soon guided me towards the Hospital Gurney and asked me to take my Pink Robe off and trousers and lay on the Gurney. I then realised that the Nurse wanted me to be completely naked on the hospital Gurney. The Nurse explained to me that she would leave the room and I would undress and then I would lay on the Gurney and cover the lower half of my Body with a Blue linen Sheet. Nurse Patterson left the room and I did as instructed and undressed and then I lay upon the Gurney and covered the lower part of my body with the Blue Linen Sheet. After a good few minutes of laying on the Hospital Gurney thinking of what was going to happen to me, I heard the door open and in walked 2 nurses wearing Red and Pink Surgical scrubs and a Doctor in Yellow scrubs with a long white lab coat on and had a yellow stethoscope around her neck and had a Yellow hairpin through her dark brown Hair. The female Doctor also had Glasses on that where dark pink and the three ladies that had entered the room where very Beautiful.

The Doctor introduced herself as Doctor Beesley and she was Anaesthetist I would be having a nice long sleep very shortly. As the Doctor was talking to me the Nurses put the side-rails up on the Gurney and put Hospital wrist restraints around my Wrists and then they restrained my wrists to the side of the Hospital Gurney side-rails, and then my Ankles where restrained as well.

Then once the Nurses had restrained me to the Gurney they set about putting Medical Equipment on the upper half of my Body. The Doctor told me that I had been restrained so I didn't fall of the Hospital Gurney and they wanted me to relax. The Nurses put a Blood Pressure Cuff around my right upper Arm and put a blood oxygen monitor on my finger to measure how much oxygen is in my Blood. Then one of the Nurses attached 3 sticky pads to my chest and then connected three wires to the sticky pads. I knew this was an ECG monitor and would listen to my Heart as I had just had an ECG in the Medical Assessment Suite. Then one of the Nurses put an I.V Canula in the back of my left hand and then attached a Drip to the canula port that had been inserted into my left hand. After connecting me to the Medical Equipment the Doctor asked me to lay my head back against the Gurney and I would be prepared for Intensive Relaxation.

I layered my head back against the Gurney and then Doctor Beesley told me that I was going to have a nice sleep and when I woke up I would be unable to talk as there would be an Endotracheal Tube down my throat and into my windpipe which make even the slightest sound impossible. Then the Doctor went to the I.V stand and put an injection Needle with white liquid into the I.V port on the I.V Drip. The Doctor told the Nurses that she loves using Propofol which is a quick Sedative and is used to Comatose Patients and Nurses call it the Milk of the Gods.

After the Doctor injected the Propofol into the I.V Drip, she then came back to the head of the Hospital Gurney and placed an Anaesthetist Face mask over my face and I was asked to take deep breaths. As I breathed in the Doctor squeezed on a Ambu Bag that was connected to the face mask and then I felt my eyelids closing and then my eyelids closed and I had been sedated.

Then the Doctor and the two Nurses prepared me for my stay in Intensive Relaxation Unit. Once the Doctor was satisfied that all the Medical Equipment was secured to me. The three health care professionals wheeled me out of the Preparation room and making sure all the Equipment that was connected to me was stable. I now had an Endotracheal Tube down my throat and one of the Nurses job was to ventilate me using an Ambu bag while they moved me down the corridor to the Intensive Relaxation Suite where I would be relaxing during my therapy at the Great Spa of Aurora.

Intensive Relaxation Suite

I opened my eyes and once my eyes focused I could see a pink ceiling with spot lights staring down at me. Once I opened my eyes I then felt something down my throat and when I looked downwards I saw a Tube entering my Mouth and was pale Blue corrugated hoses connected to the tube and I realised I was on a Medical breathing Ventilator and I couldn't feel myself breathing.

I tried to move my hands and take the tube out of my throat and found that my hands had been restrained so I couldn't remove the Breathing tube from my throat. I must have sounded an alarm as two Nurses came into the room as well as Doctor Beesley that I remembered when I was in the preparation suite. The Doctor came to the head of the Hospital Bed and leaned over and told me to relax as my Body was now in complete control of the Medical Equipment and she was very pleased about my relaxed state I was now in. I tried to say something and I then realised I couldn't make a sound with the Endotracheal tube in my throat and I could feel something inflated in my windpipe.

Doctor Beesley saw I was trying to say something and she fingered the Endotracheal tube and told me that I would be unable to speak while the Breathing tube was in my throat and the Doctor told me that there was an inflated cuff at the base of the Endotracheal tube to create Air tight seal and I would be able to feel the inflated cuff in my windpipe. The Doctor then told me that the Breathing tube will irritate at first but I would soon adjust to the breathing tube that down my throat.

After the Doctor talked to me I looked down my body as best as I could and started noticing other medical equipment that was attached to me as well as being inside of me.

I saw that there was a red tube going into my Nose and I felt it pass through my sinus and then down back of my throat and felt the tube go all the way down to my Stomach. The Doctor saw that I was looking at myself as best as I could at the Medical equipment attached and told one of the Nurses to explain all the Medical Equipment to me when the Doctor was happy enough I was fully relaxed as possible. Doctor Beesley left the room with one of the Nurses and then the other Nurse came to the head of the bed and leaned over and smiled at me and introduced herself as Rebecca and told me she was my Intensive relaxation Nurse for my stay in the Relaxation Suite. I could tell she was a lovely Nurse as she gently caressed my face and then made sure all the Medical equipment was attached to me securely. Then Rebecca started to tell me about all the Medical Equipment that I was attached to. She started at my head and told me that on my forehead was small sticky electrodes that are used to monitor my brain waves. In my Nose was a feeding tube that went down to my stomach. In my mouth was Endotracheal tube that went into my windpipe and the breathing tube was connected to a Ventilator that was controlling my breathing. Also in my mouth was endotracheal tube holder with a bite-guard so I couldn't bite on the endotracheal tube and stop the Airway. In my neck was I.V canula that was connected to a drip and on my chest I had sticky pads connected with wires which was an ECG. On my right upper arm I had a Blood pressure cuff monitoring my Blood Pressure. On my right hand finger I had a blood oxygen peg on my finger to measure the oxygen in my Blood. In my left arm I had a canula and they were connected to a Dialysis machine that was cleaning my Blood for me and making my Blood Pure. Both of my Arms had restraints at the wrists so I wouldn't injure myself while being connected to the Ventilator or the Medical Equipment. Then the Nurse told me that under the Blue Blanket covering a part of my lower part of my body was a Foley Catheter that had been inserted up my Urethra and then into my Bladder and has an inflation cuff to keep the catheter in place. This explained why I am constantly urinating as I now find out I had a Foley catheter in my Bladder. I had a canula in my right thigh that went to the dialysis machine and then the Nurse told me that on my legs I had a pair of compression boots that inflate and deflate and helps with my body circulation. After the nurse explained all the Medical Equipment to me, she then fluffed up my pillow for me and told me she would be behind the Glass window looking at the Medical Monitors and I was encouraged to relax and enjoy the experience of being in Intensive Relaxation Therapy.

Intensive Relaxation Therapy Suite, Great Spa of Auror

Ashokan Farewell

I had spent 3 days in Intensive Relaxation Suite and my body was very relaxed and Doctor Beesley was very happy with my relaxed condition. At the end of the third day in the Intensive relaxation suite Dr Bessley came with a Nurse and told me that I had finished my treatment in the Intensive Relaxation Suite and I was going to have a nice sleep and when I woke up I would be in a relaxation suite and the Ventilator and medical equipment that I was attached to would be removed.

The Doctor once again injected the white liquid into the I.V port and then Propofol was running threw my veins and I fell into a beautiful bliss state and fell a sleep. I had a dream that I was standing next to a Glass tank with a Red Spotted Octopus in it and I was playing a Violin and as I was playing Ashokan Farewell the Octopus moved around the Tank. When I stopped playing this piece of Music the Octopus stopped moving and just looked at me through the glass water tank. I played Ashokan Farewell for ages and I loved watching the Giant Red Octopus moving in the Glass Water Tank, I thought the Red Spotted Octopus was Beautiful.

The Ashokan Farewell, The Dream

81

Relaxation Suite, The Great Spa of Aurora

I woke up in a bed in a medical room and I noticed that the medical room looked a bit like a railway carriage. I must off set of an alarm as a Nurse came into the Medical room and made sure I was fine. To my surprise it was Nurse Patterson, once she looked over me and made sure I was fine and then told me I was indeed on a railway carriage and we where going to the Spa of Eusebius which is a very beautiful Spa in Aurora. I noticed I was still connected to some medical machines but the I.V lines and breathing tube had gone. My throat was very soar from having the breathing tube down my throat. Nurse Patterson gave me a bowl of ice chips and they soothed my throat so I could talk to her. Nurse Patterson told me that my Body had been completely rested and I was going to the Spa of Eusebius for more relaxation. Then Nurse Patterson took my blood pressure and also took my temperature and shone a light in my eye to make sure my eyes where fine. I was still connected to an ECG machine that was measuring my Heart rhythm and I could hear the ECG machine bleeping and was nice to listen to my Heart.

After about an hour or two in the Medical room the Nurse started removing all the medical equipment that was still on me and then the Nurse helped me up out of the hospital bed and it took me a while to find my feet and then the Nurse helped me to the bathroom where a hot bath was waiting for me with lots of bubbles. I had a nice hot bath and had took the bowl of ice chips with me as my throat was still soar. Once I had my hot bath there was a pink robe waiting for me to put on with a red waistband with a dark pink cord to tie the waistband with. After I put my pink robe on I made my way back into the medical room where a breakfast had been prepared for me and I enjoyed drinking the pure cold orange juice. My favourite part of this breakfast was having a bacon toastie with brown sauce which I enjoyed eating. While I was eating my breakfast I noticed that the train had come to a stop. Nurse Patterson noticed I saw the Train had stopped and told me that we had reached the Spa of Eusebius and was now time for me depart the Train and go to the Spa of Eusebius. While the Nurse was tae77lking to me she handed me a Yellow folder with Nicholas written on it. After breakfast the Nurse helped me to my feet and gave me the Yellow Folder and told me to give to the Therapists at the Spa of Eusebius. I took the yellow folder under my Arm and then Nurse Patterson helped me to the steps of the Carriage and when I got outside I was in for a big surprise. The Train was a Steam Locomotive from the American Wild West, I think about

1876. The colours on the Locomotive was amazing and was very stunning to look at. The Wild West Locomotive was named Eusebius and the train had pulled into a train station and the name of station was called Aurora. On the opposite side of the train station was a path that lead to the Spa of Eusebius. I decided to follow the path away from the Train Station and make my way to the Spa of Eusebius. Nurse Patterson was right my Body was fully rested and I felt very relaxed. I remember my time in the Intensive Relaxation Suite and being connected to all the different medical machines.

Spa of Eusebius Train Station, Great Spa of Aurora

Entrance to the Spa of Eusebius, Great Spa of Aurora

Entrance to the Spa of Eusebius

I followed the Path and long the way I took in the Beautiful bright coloured flowers that where on display on route to the Spa of Eusebius. I come to what I can describe as a sandstone temple and there was a lady in a Purple kimono dress with a Metallic purple and Gold waistband that over-lapped at the front where the lady put her arms through. To the left of the sandstone temple was a square fish pond and then far left was a red Brick wall covered in array of Flowers. The whole area of the sandstone temple was covered in bright coloured flowers and there was also a bright coloured Chariot Cart that was to the right of the sandstone temple. When I got closer to the sandstone temple I could see Red sign above the 2 wooden doors reading the Spa of Eusebius.

The lady greeted me at the steps of the Spa of Eusebius and welcomed me to the Spa. The lady introduced herself as Chloe and asked if I could follow her to the reception through the wooden doors of this sandstone temple and then I would be greeted by other Therapists within the Spa. I handed Chloe my Yellow folder that Nurse Patterson had given to me on the Train and then before I followed Chloe into the Temple via the wooden doors. I took a look at all the beautiful flowers that where on display at the steps of the Spa of Eusebius. I enjoyed looking at the Blue and Yellow Chariot, it was very stunning. Then Chloe took my hand and then we pushed the two wooden doors and we entered the Spa of Eusebius. As we walked through the wooden doors I wondered what treatments I would be having in the Spa of Eusebius.

Make-up Suite at the Spa of Eusebius

Me and Chloe went through the two Wooden doors and I entered the Spa of Eusebius. When we entered the Spa there was a Nurse in Pink Surgical scrubs and a therapist in a purple Kimono. The Lady Therapist in the Purple Kimono introduced herself and the therapist name was Angela and the Nurse name was Susan. Both the Nurse and the therapist ushered me into a room and was asked to take a seat in a Make-up chair. I handed the therapist the Yellow Folder with my name on it and then I took a seat in the Make-up Chair. Once I sat in the make-up chair, Susan the Nurse started putting make-up on my face and Neck. First a foundation base was applied to my Neck and Face. Then I had mascara put on my eyelashes, and blue eye shadow on my eyelids. Next to my surprise I had Blue Lipstick put on my Lips. Once the make-up was done the therapist and the Nurse decided to put a Yellow Flower in my Hair that went over my Glasses. Then the Therapist Angela asked me to take my Pink robe off and the waist band that was tied around my waist and the therapist then told me that I had a new Garment to wear.

I took my Pink robe off and then the therapist handed me a white and red Roman toga, and the Nurse and the Therapist helped me put on the Roman Toga. Once I had my Toga on the Nurse then handed me a Paint Brush with Blue Paint on the tip of the Brush and I was asked to create symbols on a Yellow canvas that the Nurse held up for me. I was very happy and content with my Yellow Flower in my Hair and make-up with my Roman Toga on. Then he therapist Angela asked me to follow her to my first Treatment at the Spa of Eusebius, I was getting excited as to what my first treatment was going to be at the Spa of Eusebius. The Therapist Angela could see I was getting excited and told me that I would be having some very relaxing treatments and she was positive that I would enjoy them. We walked along a Beautiful coloured corridor with lots of Flowers. While walking down the corridor I told Angela all about my stay in the Intensive Relaxation suite and that I had a breathing tube down my throat and was connected to all kinds of Medical Equipment, Angela told me Intensive Relaxation Suite allows your Body complete Rest.

Make-up Suite at the Spa of Eusebius

The Tree of Light, Spa of Eusebius

We got to the end of the Corridor and walked outside into a court yard with a Grass lawn. In the middle of the court-yard was a Blue Tree with lights wrapped around the Blue tree. It was now Night time and the Night Sky of Aurora was very Beautiful. I felt relaxed in my Roman Toga and I had Blue lipstick on. The Therapist Angela told me to wait in this court-yard and my next therapist would be with me shortly. Then Angela left the court-yard and I stood there watching the lights shining from the Blue Tree. On the opposite side of the court-yard was a Roman Stone statue with a man holding up a Sword at an Angle. I watched the light of the Blue Tree for along time, I felt as if I was at the Centre of the Universe when I looked at the Blue Tree that I now called the Tree of Light. I decided to sit on the Grass and looked at the Tree of Light and the Night Sky of Aurora. In the Night Sky of Aurora I could see distance Planets and Suns that where far away. I thought to myself that why wouldn't there be a Blue Tree at the Centre of the Universe.

The Tree of Light branched looked as if they where branches to different Galaxies and different Worlds and Cultures. I sat on the Grass and bonded with the Tree of Light. I understood why I had Blue lipstick on as when I spoke the Tree of Light started moving, and the Blue Tree movement caused sounds which where in perfect harmony with the Universe. The Tree of Light had a circular wooden barrier around it as I understood the Tree was very Fragile.

The Tree of Light, The Spa of Eusebius

Vacuum Therapy Treatment/Hypoxi

while I was sitting on the Grass next to the Tree of Light, a Nurse walked up to me and introduced herself as Louise and asked me to follow her to my next Therapy treatment. I had enjoyed being with the Tree of Light and I really wanted to sit with the Tree of Light for a lot longer but the Nurse gently persuaded me to go with her to my next Therapy treatment.

The both of us walked out the Courtyard and left the Tree of Light behind us. The Nurse took me along a series of Corridors until we came to a room that read 'Vacuum Therapy/Hypoxi' written on the Door. The Nurse opened the Door to the Vacuum Therapy Room and we both walked into the Therapy room and I was lost for breathe as to what I saw in the Room. In the Centre of the Room was a Hospital Bed and next to the Hospital Bed was Medical monitors and monitoring leads on the other side of the room was a large machine with lots of Blue hoses coming out of the Machine and there was different glass Gauges on the front of the machine below the Blue Hoses. The Nurse told me that the Medical machine was Vacuum suction/Hypoxi therapy unit and I first needed to put on a Hypoxi vacuum Suit.

The Nurse then helped me into a Hypoxi suit which looked very similar to a Drysuit worn by Scuba Divers. The suit was orange in Colour and had attachments where I presumed the Blue hoses attach to the suit sockets. Before putting the Hypoxi suit fully on, the Nurse put ECG electrodes on my chest so she could Monitor my Heart rate while I was having Hypoxi Therapy treatment. After I put the Hypoxi suit on the Nurse then helped me lay on the Hospital Bed and when I comfortable the Nurse started connecting the Blue hoses to the Hypoxi suit that I was wearing. When the Nurse was happy that all the blue tubes where connected to the Suit, she then came to the Head of the bed and started connecting electrodes to my head. Which was to monitor my Brain activity during the therapy session. Then the Nurse told me she was going to start the vacuum therapy machine and I would feel suction all over my Body and it would be a strange sensation at first. The Nurse started the Vacuum Therapy Machine and I definitely felt the Suction as the Air was taken out of the Suit.

The Nurse after switching and the Vacuum Therapy machine, then switched on the Medical monitors that would monitor my Vitals signs during the Suction Therapy. Then the Nurse put Ear plugs in my Ears, and then I couldn't hear anything as well as covering my eyes with a dark mask so I couldn't see anymore. I lay there in silence on the Hospital Bed and I was totally blind with only the feeling of the Vacuum Suction to keep me company. My senses had been taken away from me and I lay there in a blissful silence and the feeling of the Hypoxi Vacuum Suction on my Body.

Vacuum Therapy Treatment at Spa of Eusebius

Cactus Therapy Treatment at Spa of Eusebius

I don't know how long I was in the Vacuum therapy session, I think it might have been a couple of hours or maybe more. Nurse Louise helped me out of the hypoxi suit and took off all the Medical wires that where attached to my Body during Vacuum Therapy session. The Nurse then helped me back into my Red and white roman toga and then she asked me to sit on the hospital bed and wait for my next therapist. I did as instructed and sat on the hospital Bed and waited for my next therapist to arrive. My next therapist was a lady named Alisha and my next therapy would be a Cactus Massage. I was asked to follow the therapist to the treatment area. We arrived at the treatment area and the room had a Asian feel to it and I could breathe in the fresh Air of the outside World. The therapist helped me take my roman Toga off and then I lay face down on a therapy table and the therapist covered the lower part of my Body with a White Sheet. I was very relieved when I found out that the Cactus Massage didn't involve the Spines of a Cactus leaf that would of pierced my Skin. My Cactus massage used Nopal Cactus

89

paddles that directed Meringue to the skin and makes you feel rejuvenated and helps to remove toxins and re-hydrate my Skin.

Cactus Massage Therapy, Spa of Eusebius

Shaman Drumming, Tree of Light

After the Cactus massage, Alisha took me back to the Tree of Light where it was now Daylight. Alisha told me to wait by the Tree for my next therapy to begin. Then Alisha left and I once again stood in wonder next to the Tree of Light. My next therapist arrived a couple of minutes after the therapist Alisha had left and my new therapist name was Maria, and she would be taken me on a spiritual using Shaman Drums. We both made our way to another part of the Courtyard where there was four standing stones. On the smaller standing Stones were two Native American Headdress for me and the therapist Maria to Wear. The Therapist Maria was wearing a White Japanese Kimono and a white Obi Belt and she looked very Beautiful in her White Kimono. Also by the smaller standing Stones where two Shaman Drums and I thought I might be learning to play this very shortly. The Therapist and I put the Indian Headdresses on and picked up the Shaman Drums, and Maria showed me how to play a Shaman Drum. Suddenly we get a rhythm going and on the other side of the Courtyard the Tree of Light was producing lots of different colours and the Tree of Light moved in Harmony with our drumming as both opened our Hearts to the Beautiful Tree of Light.

Shaman Drumming, Tree of Light, Spa of Eusebius

Arched Wooden Doorway, Spa of Eusebius

I had reached Spiritual Enlightenment with the Therapist Maria and I had enjoyed my Shaman drumming Therapy session. After the Shaman drumming the Therapist Maria told me that my time at the Spa of Eusebius had come to an end and it was time for me to go back to the Black and White World but not before there was one last surprise for me in the Spa of Eusebius. Maria led me to another Courtyard past the Tree of Light and then she opened a metal Gate and I found myself in another Courtyard where there was a orange Rug and laying on the Orange Rug was Indian Sitar.

To the right of the Orange Rug was a big Glass Window where I could see the bathroom where I had started my journey back to the Great Spa of Aurora. The big glass window was also a reminder that the Black and White World was waiting for me.

91

Next to the Big Glass Window was an Arched Wooden Door and next to the Arched Wooden door was a coloured pane of Glass that looked very Beautiful. In front of the Arched wooden Door was a set of steps leading to the Tomb of Eusebius, which was an Egyptian Coffin. I decided to sit on the Orange Rug and play the Indian Sitar. At this point Maria left me alone in the Courtyard and told me that the Arched Wooden door was ready for me to open when I felt like going back to the Black and White World. I sat on the Orange Rug playing the Indian Sitar with a Yellow Flower in my Hair.

When suddenly a Bright Light shone above the Arched Wooden Door and I could make out it was a Cup of some kind. I put the Indian Sitar on the Orange Rug and made my way over to the Bright Light and the Cup that was above the Arched Wooden Doorway. When I got nearer to the Cup, I realised what it was and I knew I had to go through the Arched wooden door back to the Black and White World. I opened the Arched wooden door and could see my Bedroom and then I stepped through the Arched wooden Door and walked into my Bedroom. I began to realise what the Dialysis Machine was for when I was in the Intensive Relaxation Suite at the Spa of Aurora. The Dialysis machine was making my Blood Pure so the Cup would reveal itself to me and I would understand Pure enlightenment at the Spa of Eusebius. I have enjoyed my Return Journey to the Great Spa of Aurora and I was now back in my Bedroom looking at my Yellow Flower.

Arched Wooden Doorway, The Spa of Eusebius

The Chronicles

The Chronicles is Nicholas Adventures while writing his Autobiography The Spiral Staircase that was his 3 Year Adventures doing over 100 different Adventures from February 2010 to May 2013.

Gyrocopter Experience, York, 25th May 2013

Me and Mum arrived at the Airfield in Rufforth near York at 11am, it had taken us 2 hours to drive from Wallasey to York. I was two hours earlier for my Gyrocopter flight experience, so we went to the Cafe next to the Gyrocopter hanger and had two coffee's, we drank the Coffee on the picnic tables outside the Cafe. The Sun was shining and me and Mum where enjoying the Sun while drinking our coffee. As we sat drinking our Coffee we watched Airplanes and microlights taking off and landing. While watching the Planes I realised I was getting Sun Burnt, so I decided to sit in the shade for 30 minutes. It was soon time for the gyrocopter flight. The instructor name was phil and gave me and Mum a tour of the Gyrocopter Hanger and showed us some old Gyrocopter's from 20 years ago. After the tour of the Gyrocopter Hanger the instructor gave me a padded flying suit and I put the flying suit on and then Phil the instructor put his flying sit on and then the instructor and myself made our way over to the Gyrocopter. The Gyrocopter was white in colour and had a engine on the Back with a propeller attached to the engine and above was set of helicopter blades. There where two seats on the Gyrocopter, the seat in front was for the instructor and I sat in the second seat behind the instructor. I got into the Gyrocopter second seat and the instructor handed me the crash Hat I was to wear for the Gyrocopter flight experience.

After helping me strap myself in the instructor got in the front seat and then the instructor put his crash on and then spoke to me using the microphones built into the Crash hats. By this point I was very excited but I held it together and I was sensible and enjoying the experience. To my surprise we started taxi down the Runway and the instructor told me it doesn't take off like a Helicopter. A Gyrocopter takes off like a Plane using a Runway, the propeller at the back of the Gyrocopter pushes it forward and top blades rotate with the wind resistance created by the Propeller.

Once we got clearance from the Control tower the instructor opened the throttle of the Gyrocopter and we started moving fast down the runway, then suddenly we where flying, I saw the ground below me and could hear the engine behind me and I felt the Vibrations of the Gyrocopter. The instructor took the gyrocopter up 1500ft and we flew over the out-skirts of York, and I saw York Minister from the Gyrocopter. We flew over lush Green fields and I could see as far as the eye could see. I had chosen a great day to come as the visibility was amazing. We flew over Rivers and went really close to the water and followed the twist and turns of the River. I was really enjoying my Gyrocopter experience it was a lovely sunny day as well. We also flew over ponds and I was taking photographs using my camera. I enjoyed the Air hitting my face and the sense of freedom from the World below me and I was very happy in the Gyrocopter.

Soon the instructor turned back towards the Airfield and the instructor let me fly the Gyrocopter, I was a bit nervous at first taking control of the Gyrocopter but found flying the Gyrocopter a lot of fun and I was steering left and right and following the Instructor instructions on where to fly the Gyrocopter. After about 20 minutes of me flying the Gyrocopter the instructor took over from me and then we flew to the runway. On the way to the Runway the instructor showed me some stunts in the Gyrocopter and we also did a fly-by above the runway. After the stunts and the fly-by the instructor landed the gyrocopter and then we taxi back to the Gyrocopter Hangar. The instructor took my photograph of me in the Gyrocopter and then I got out of the Gyrocopter and shook his hand and thanked him for the experience. In the hangar Mum was waiting for me and gave me a big hug and told me how brave I was flying in a Gyrocopter. I had really enjoyed the experience of flying in a Girocopter. After the Girocopter flight me and Mum made our way back home to Wallasey. On the way back home I told Mum all about the Girocopter flight and I told Mum I got to fly it as well.

26th May 2013, Queen Dock, Liverpool

I arrived at Queen Dock at 9:15am and made my way down the stairs to the Jetty below Queen Dock Water-sport Centre. I had come to Queen dock in Liverpool to do a two mile swim which is about Six circuits of the Dock. I met up with other swimmers this morning and told them about my Gyrocopter flight the Day before. After talking with my swimming friends I got myself ready to swim. I am a Open water swimmer and I have swum in Open Water for 10 years and I love swimming in the outdoors and the freedom that the Sport of open water swimming gives me,, I love swimming and I have swam since I was 4 years old and I have loved the water ever since. In open water swimming we use a pair of swimming trunks, Swimming goggles, swim cap and Vaseline we use for under the Arms to stop abrasion. The start of the Open water swimming season starts in March and it can be quite cold but all the open water swimmers love this time of year. I swum 2 miles this morning and I really enjoyed my swim this morning, after my swim I had a Shower and then got changed and had a drink of Coffee from my flask. Then I talked with other swimmers about swimming at Eccleston ferry near Chester which is a beautiful place swim on a nice sunny evening in the Summer months. Eccleston is quite village in Cheshire and is a very tranquill place to swim. The water temperature this morning I think was about 12 oC and the sun was out as well.

27th May 2013

Me and my brother Lee and Mum went to the Aquarium shop to buy 4 fish for our fish pond. We went to Andy's Aquatics in New Ferry and I got really excited when we got to the Fish Shop. Andy's Aquatics had a range of cold water fish, tropical fish and Saltwater Fish. I spent ages looking at the Clown fish tank and saying "i want a Nemo Fish". I have found out that a Clown Fish (Nemo) uses a Salt water tank and is very specialised to look after. Me and my Brother Lee looked at the Tropical Fish and thought about what to put in our tropical fish tank that we share together. I would like to put in a Blue Lobster as I think there Great. After looking at the tropical fish we went outside and looked at the cold water fish. I decided I would have 4 Shubunkins fish that where Blue with colourful spots. I chose the 4 Shubinkins that I wanted and the shop assistant got the Shubinkins that I liked and put them in a Bag for me containing Water. Once I got the Fish Mum drove us home and I held onto the fish, I was really excited about putting my fish in the Pond. We got home and I went to the pond and put the Bag in the pond and after 10 minutes Me and Mum opened the bag and the Fish swam away into the Pond.

28th May 2013, My Birthday

My Birthday started at Synexus Medical Research in Crosby, Liverpool. I was having blood tests taken for chorestal study, throughout the study I will be having ECG done and my Blood pressure and furthered blood tests. After my Blood with synexus I had my Hair cut at the Barber's, my hair had become a mess and not being able to comb my Hair anymore I got it cut short so I can manage my Hair. At midday I had a visit from Psychiatric Nurse to see how I was, I was very happy today and was enjoying my Birthday. At 1:30pm Dad got ready and put his coat on and then we went out to look at a New Car for me. The Car I had chosen is a Honda Jazz EX with semi Automatic Gear Box, Panoramic roof, Cruise control, front fog headlights and the Colour I wanted was Blue.

We got to the Honda Centre at Cheshire Oaks, Ellesmereport and I took my New Car for a test drive, the Honda Jazz was amazing to drive it is a very futuristic Car. I fell in Love with this Honda Jazz Ex i-shirt. After the test drive we went home and we had my Birthday Tea which was a Mix Grill and I had my Birthday Cake which was Chocolate Cake. After my Birthday I opened my Birthday cards and Birthday presents I got a New tent for camping from my Mum and Dad and Lee got me a Pillow with built in Speakers, and Mum friend Helen got me a Budweiser Beer t-shirt. I had really enjoyed today it has been a great Birthday and enjoyed test Driving my New Car.

1st June 2013

swum 4 mile swim in Liverpool Docks in 2 hours 22 minutes in the Ivan Percival Open Water swimming Championship.
Enjoyed drinking Wychwood Beer and watching Steven Speilberg Lincoln Film.

2nd June 2013

My Shoulder (left) was grazed by Abrasion and was very sore indeed, I had Sun stroke and had to spend today in the shade.

5th June 2013

I had my counselling appointment with my Councillor at the Stein Centre, Birkenhead. I talked about my new Adventures and I am really excited about my new Car and showed my councillor my New Samsung Galaxy S2 smartphone.

8th June 2013

Went to a Burlesque Show in New Brighton and enjoyed watching the ladies doing a Fan Dance and getting nearly naked on the stage, it was great Fun.

9th June 2013

This evening I drove my Honda Jazz EX i-shift to Cinema (VUE) at Cheshire Oaks. We went to see Star Trek into Darkness. I love Star Trek films an the last Star Trek film I went to see at the Cinema was Star Trek First Contact. Star Trek into Darkness was very enjoyable and special effects where very good and there was lots of Action.

10th June 2013

Tonight I got first look at the Sony Playstation 4 Games console and I am very impressed with Sony new games console. Later I sat on my Bed watching 'Finding Nemo' with my Wizard cloak on and cuddled my Cuddly toy Dinosaur Herbert.

15th June 2013

Me and my Brother Lee arrived at Mum and Dad Caravan in Llanberis, North Wales. Me and Lee put my new tent up that I had got for my Birthday and then we camped next to Mum and Dad Caravan and during the night you could hear the River that was next to the Caravan Park.

16th June 2013

I found myself sitting in the River in a sheltered rock pool, it was a tranquil place to sit and the Water was very cold. I sat in the cold river for 25 minutes and I enjoyed watching the water flow down the river and then Lee came down to the River edge and told me that dinner was ready in the caravan.

19th June 2013

I found myself entering the River Dee with 300 other swimmers, the mud was very thick on the side of the Banks of the River. Tonight chronicles was the River Dee 2km swim. I waded through the Mud and before I got stuck in the Mud. I plunged forward and entered the River Dee, I swum the short distance to the start of the swim and waited for the Horn for the mass swim start involving 300 swimmers. The river Dee swim was a very fast paced swim and I enjoyed the sprint finish at the end of the swim. I got cramp in my left leg towards the end of the swim and I had to be helped out of the water. After I got out by the Suspension bridge I drank my can of coke that every swimmer was given, the coke got rid of any bad Bacteria that I might of swallowed. I got changed with my swimming friend and had a lot of laugh's and we talked about the swim. I had enjoyed swimming the River Dee and swimming with my friends. The Water temperature for the swim was good at 18 degrees. After I got changed I made my way across Chester Suspension Bridge and then to the Groves where I had parked my Honda Jazz EX. I drove home and I was still excited from doing the swim. The Sun had been shining all day and it was a Beautiful Evening to Swim.

24th June 2013

There was a lot of Jellyfish in the Dock, the Jellyfish we have in Queen Dock are Moon Jellyfish and start a couple of inches big at the start of the Swim Season in May and can grow about a foot across by the end of the Summer. Tonight I swum 5 laps of Queen Dock and I though the water was quite warm tonight. The weather was cloudy and there was a slight breeze on the water. After I swam the 5 laps of the Dock I got out and had a cup of coffee, Jenny one of the other swimmers made some nice Cake, which I enjoyed eating with my cup of coffee. After I got changed I talked about the Zip Wire in North Wales I was going to do in July 2013.

26th June 2013

Dad took me down to New Brighton so I could with my remote control Cars. I started at Brighton where I played with my Nikko Vapourizer Car that works on Water. After I played with the Nikko Vapourizer I then played with my Carson Rock Crawler which is a remote control that climbs up rocks. I then played with my remote control FTX Brushless 2.4ghz Buggy which can reach speeds if up to 30 mph. I enjoyed playing with my remote control Cars tonight and when we got home I put my remote control Cars back in the Cupboard under my Bed.

27th June 2013

I looked at myself in the Mirror at the BDSM Club on Merseyside, I had a Georgian Dress on and Marion Antoinette Wig on. I thought I looked very beautiful in my Burgundy Georgian dress, I used a Spanish Fan to cool myself as the costume was very hot to wear and I had to keep cooling myself down using my fan as I also had a Corset as well, which was very restrictive. My favourite toy at the club is a swing mounted on the ceiling and I love sitting in the swing and there is a big mirror in front of the swing, so I can see myself in the Mirror.

29th June 2013

I have ordered myself a remote control Boat this afternoon it is a Remote control Hydroplane boat which is two and half feet long and   reach speed of 25mph. I am also looking at getting a Nikko Aqua splitter r/c Boat. The Sun was shining today and Dad was hard at work making a new garden pond. I have asked Dad if I can get a Dwarf Sturgeon Fish for new pond.

30th June 2013

I sold my Nissan Micra Car today and I made sure my old Car went to a good home. My Nissan Micra was sold to someone starting out in the Motoring World. I did have a tear in my eye as my Nissan Micra SX was driven away from me for the last time. I enjoyed driving the Nissan Micra SX for the last 4 years and has served me well. I have now got a Honda Jazz EX i-shift I love it to bits. My new Car is electric blue and is the best colour Honda made the Honda Jaz in. I will remember all the good times I had in the Nissan Micra SX and now I have a New Car for my new Adventures.

6th July 2013

Dad was taking me on the motorbike to the Caravan at Llanberis, North Wales. Mum my Brother Lee where already at the Caravan and we would go on Dad Motorbike which is a Yamaha XVS1300 custom motorbike. I had never been on a motorbike before and I had been looking forward today experience. I got on the back of the motorbike behind Dad and got myself ready for 80 mile journey to the Caravan. Riding pillion on the back of Dad motorcycle was an amazing experience. You feel the whole energy of the motorbike working. At Colwyn Bay we stopped off at Colywn Bay Honda Motorbike shop and we looked at all the motorbikes they had on sale. After looking at the motorbike shop we then set towards the Caravan on A55 coastal road. The scenery was very beautiful I got a good view of the Sea and the countryside of North Wales. We arrived at the caravan at 5pm and Mum was cooking the tea and I then told Mum and Lee about my experience of being on Dad motorbike. I had really enjoyed riding pillion on Dad motorbike today.

7th July 2013

I found myself this morning looking at the Train Station in Anglesey with the Longest name. I couldn't make out the name or understanding it's meaning and it was a very pretty Railway station. Next to the Train station was Department store called James Pringle Weaver and above the sign in english translation of the meaning of the train station name. Which is 'St Marys Church in the Hollow of the White Hear to the Rapid whirlpool of Llantysilio of the Red Cave'. I think the true meaning of the name of this train station is buried deep within the Heart of the Welsh people and will remain a mystery. After visiting the Train station with the longest name in the World, I decided when I got back to the Caravan I would go for a swim in the sheltered Pool in the River. I got back to the Caravan and put my swim costume on and then made my way to the River. I got into a sheltered rock pool in the river and the water was very refreshing and I sat in the sheltered rock pool and watched the River run past me. I decided to arch my back against a small waterfall and let the water massage my back. Soon ii was dinner-time and Lee came and got me from the river and then we both walked back to the Caravan.

13th July 2013

I went shopping this morning and got some crisps for tonight, I was going to watch a Samurai movie called Hara Kiri, Death of a Samurai. Which I have been looking forward to watching. I love Japanese movies. My favourite Samurai movie is 13 Assassins which contains an hour Sword fight with 13 Samurai's against over 300 Samurai's, this is a great Samurai film. I have still yet to see 1954 film Seven Samurai's which was later remade as the Magnificent Seven by Hollywood.

13th July 2013, Evening

I got my swim Bag ready for tomorrow Across Mersey River Swim. I washed my swim goggles and made sure I had a swim costume for tomorrow swim. I always get nervous before Across Mersey River swim as I have no idea what the Tide is going to be like.

I enjoy drinking a Pint of Wychwood Goliath Ruby Ale that I get from Home and Bargain and I love the taste of Wychwood Hobgoblin ruby Ale as well. I have looked on there Website and I got excited when I looked and saw they have an online shop with lots of exciting gifts.

14th July 2013

I took my place on the Slipway at cockle shell bay on the Liverpool side of the River Mersey. I was standing on the slipway with another 89 swimmers. We where all waiting for the word that we could all enter the Water and prepare to swim across the River Mersey. Once we where given the Green light we then entered the water and prepared ourselves for the swim across the river. The start whistle was blown and the race across the Mersey began. I started swimming at a good pace and I enjoyed swimming through the swell and crashing into the waves. I had a good line across the River and up to half way I was Jellyfish free and I hadn't been stung yet. Towards the end of the swim I could see the finish through my swimming goggles which was Monk ferry Slipway in Birkenhead. Just before the finish near the Slipway there is a strong current that is just in front of the slipway and I swum as fast as I could to get to the finish and then I stood on the Green roll mat and I finished the River Mersey Swim. I had again made it across the River and it still remains a very hard swim and never to be taken lightly. I really enjoyed this swim.

15th July 2013

I arrived at Queen Dock at 6pm and I got changed and went down the slipway and then I entered the water and found the temperature of the water to be quite warm, being very close to swimming pool temperature. I started swimming at a medium pace and making sure I took long strokes through the water as well as using a strong leg kick. I swum 7 laps of the 550 metre circuit and the Sun was out and I was enjoying my swimming with a pair prescription Swim Goggles.

16th July 2013

I spent the evening cleaning Pond Snails for the New pond Mum and Dad are making. Mum and Dad had left the snails in a bucket for me and I got some tissue paper and I started cleaning the Water snails Shells. I got all the duck weed off there shells and other water nasty's that had inhabited the Snail Shells. I cleaned about 70 Water snails and once I had finished cleaning the water snails, Dad let me put the Water snails in the New Pond. It was good fun watching the water snails in the Water coming out of there shells.

16th July 2013

I sat with Dad in the back Garden next to the Chimney fire. We talked about remote control motorbikes that Dad had got himself. I like sitting in front of the open fire and I watched the wood as it crackled in the fire. I asked Dad about different batteries for my remote control cars. At 10pm I went inside and poured myself a glass of Pepsi and went up stairs to my Bedroom to Watch a Movie. The Movie that I chose to watch was James Cameron Alien where Colonial Marines go to a Planet to battle Aliens and Aliens is beautiful crafted Film.

20th July 2013

I had my hand stamped as I entered the GMEX Centre to visit the Comic Convention. The Comic convention was for Comic book creators to show off there talent, trade stands as well guest appearances. Once I got my hand stamped I made my way into the Comic convention and soon found I couldn't move very far. There was a lot of people at the Convention, some people had come had come in Comic book costumes and Japanese Anime Costumes. At one stage I thought there was too many people in the Gmex Centre, Manchester , as i couldn't get to any of the stands to look at anything and I couldn't really see anything. After hour and half I decided to go outside as I was getting to hot in the Comic Convention. The people that had come in Costume had put a lot of effort into there costumes and the costumes where very good. After dinner I got my photograph taken with the Storm Troopers from Star Wars. At 3pm I decided to set off for home and I had enjoyed coming to the Comic Convention but I thought the Gmex Centre was too small to hold the convention as there was even a Queue to get out of the Comic Book Convention.

20th July 2013, Evening

Dad took me down to the Model Boating lake in New Brighton to try my new remote control hydroplane boat. My hydroplane boat was quite fast on the Lake and I enjoyed playing with my Hydroplane Boat. Then we went to B&Q car park for about 8:30pm when it was empty to try Dad's new remote control Brushless Sport Bike. The brushless sport bike was very fast and it took a while to get use to the controls.

21st July 2013

I spent the morning in a Kayak doing the Safety cover for the swimmers in Queen Dock. At the end of the swim session I decided to see if I could still Eskimo Roll a kayak and I found out that I couldn't eskimo roll a Kayak and found myself doing a capsize drill just by the slipway at Queen Dock. I had enjoyed kayaking this morning and I had a lot of fun getting wet.

27th July 2013

I have come for a week Holiday at Mum and Dad caravan, and today me and Mum went to the Butterfly farm on Anglesey. The Butterflies where kept in a tropical glass house and the tropical glass house contained all kinds of different coloured Butterflies. The Butterflies had lots of bright colours and I even saw a Blue winged Butterfly that was very Beautiful. The Butterfly farm also had 2 Kunkune Pigs which I thought where great and tickled the back of there ears. After going to the Butterfly farm we went to a Beauty Spot on the east side of Anglesey and me and Mum had a picnic by the Sea on a wooden picnic table. Once we had dinner we went to the Spinnies a Bird nature reserve just by the City of Bangor, North Wales. I had come to the Spinnies to see if I could see a Kingfisher Bird with beautiful Blue and Yellow markings. I never saw a Kingfisher bird and at 3pm we went back to the Caravan and I put my New tent up that I had been given for my Birthday. Dad helped me peg out the Tent and then we had tea which was fish cakes, boiled potatoes and chocolate Cake.

28th July 2013

Dad showed me a Deep pool in the River next to the Caravan. I decided this afternoon to have a swim in the Deep Pool a short walk from the caravan. I got to the Deep Pool by the River and lay my Towel, T-shirt and shorts on a large Rock next to the Deep Pool. I took my prescription swim goggles with me to the Deep pool that I had now Called Mermaid Rockpool. I waded into the deep Pool and then I put my whole body into the water, and at first the water was slightly cold. After a couple of minutes I adjusted to the temperature of the Water. I tried my prescription swim goggles and to my amazement I saw Rainbow trout in Mermaid Rock Pool. They where only Baby Rainbow trout about five inches long with different colours and very beautiful to watch. After Tea I decided to go snorkelling in Mermaid Rock Pool and watch the Rainbow trout swimming in the stream. Dad came to Mermaid Rock Pool and floated in the pool in a 2 man inflatable boat and dad even had a look through the Snorkel Mask and saw the Rainbow trout. Mum came to Mermaid Rock Pool as well and took a photograph of me and Dad together in Mermaid Rock Pool. I enjoyed snorkelling in Mermaid Rock Pool and loved watching the Rainbow trout swimming in the current and Dad was paddling 2 Man inflatable Boat.

29th July 2013

I parked in the car park at Llyn Padarn lake and walked across to Surf-lines outdoor centre. I had come to Llanberis to swim in the Lake called Llyn Padarn. I was hoping that I didn't need to wear a wetsuit tonight as it was quite warm. I was made up when the swim instructor Mary told me that I didn't need to wear a wetsuit and then I got changed in the changing room and got ready for the swim. I got changed and then waited with the other swimmers in shop area of Surf-lines. Then at 5:50pm we made our way to the Lake shore and then we introduced ourselves to one another and then got into the water and started swimming up the lake, with swim instructor in open Canoe for support. We swam up the lake and the scenery was very Beautiful. Through my swim goggles I could see Snowdon Mountain Range and this was quite a swimming pool to swim in, the pontoon that was by the Shore was from the rowing lake at Olympic Games in London 2012. When they where dismantling the Pontoons they gave Llanberis a section so people could swim in the lake and have lots of fun. The swim itself was very like a swim trek, swimming while taking in the Great scenery that was on offer. The swim was 1200 metres and I thought I saw a fish while I was swimming.

30th July 2013

I stood on a platform with a 500 ft drop below me. I had come to Zipworld in Bethesda, North Wales to do Europe Longest Zipwire which is a mile long. The start of the experience was getting harnessed into the equipment and then the group I was in made our way to the small Zipwire to get the feel of what the big Zipwire was goint to be like. It was soon my turn to be harnessed in ready to go down the small Zipwire. I successfully completed the small zipwire and when everyone had done the small Zipwire it was then time for the Quarry tour which was a 4x4 truck that took us to the top of the Slate Mine where the Mile Zipwire would take place. We dis-barked at the top of the slate mine and I saw the platform we would be launching from. The instructor harnessed me into the Zipwire and made sure I was secure on the Zipline and all the safety lines where connected. Then I was asked if I was ready to ride Europe Longest Zipwire and I was very ready for the Zipwire. Then the instructor pulled the cord and then I flew along the Zipwire at 90mph with a Sheer drop of 500ft. I went down the Zipwire in a cradle Harness and it was like flying threw the Air and I could feel the Air rushing past my Goggles.

3rd January 2014

I had survived the Jump into the Quarry of the Blue Lagoon and I am now in Wrexham General Hospital being kept in for Observation. Two motocross riders having a New Year's Day motorbike ride around the Quarry saw me jump into the Water and one of the motorcross riders dived into the freezing cold Pool to rescue me. I was told by the Doctors that I was very lucky I didn't hurt myself falling from that height into Water. `

Helter Skelter
Originated in the United States in an Amusement Park at Coney Island the term "helter skelter" was first recorded in the United Kindom at Blackpool Pleasure Beach in 1906.

The Clock Maker of Shillington Square
Written by Nicholas Robinson

Thomas Taylor spent his days repairing people Watches in his little Watch makers Shop in Shillington Square. Thomas had a small Window where he would watch the world go by as he repaired the Broken Watches. In his little Shop Thomas displays watches for Sale but people never bought watches from him, they only wanted there Watches Repaired.

One Day a lady walked in, and Thomas fell in Love with Her, the Lady name was Claire and went well with her long flowing Brown Hair. She asked Thomas if he could fix her watch and Thomas took a good look at the Ladies watch and told her it would be ready in a couple of Days.

Thomas took great care in repairing the Lady watch and he made her watch look good as new and then he parcelled up the Watch with a not asking would the lady like to come on a date. Two days later the Lady walked back into the Shop and undid the parcel handed to her from Thomas and gave Thomas his answer to the note written in the Parcel. The Lady told Thomas to meet her by the Clock tower at 8pm and they would go out on a Date on this very Night.

Thomas that evening was very busy with himself, getting himself ready for the date that he had with Claire and he would meet her at the Clock Tower at 8pm. Earlier in the Day Thomas had bought some flowers from the Flower stall in Shillington Square and hoped Claire would like them. Thomas put his best suit on and made is way to the Clock Tower to go out on a Date with Claire.

Thomas arrived at the Clock Tower five minutes before 8pm holding his bunch of flowers for Claire, 20 minutes past and there was no sign of Claire and it began to Rain. Thomas stood there in the Rain under the Clock Tower for hours waiting for Claire and then he realised that Claire wasn't coming. Thomas Heart was broken as he made his way back to his little Watch Shop in Shillington Square. The next day he opened his watch repair shop as usual and once again setting to work repairing people watches. Days went by as Thomas repaired the watches given to him by customers to repair and all he could think of was the Night Under the Clock Tower where his Heart was Broken. Still no one had ever bought a watch from him or asked to look at his watches on display.

Thomas Heart broken from not seeing Claire again, decided he would mend his Heart by setting to work at making Anatomical Heart out of Cogs and watch making Materials.

The Months went by for Thomas Taylor in Shillington Square, Summer turned to Winter and Night turned to Day. When not repairing customers Watches, Thomas spent his time making his Anatomical Heart that would mend his Broken Heart. Over Time the days grew shorter and Time had crept up on Thomas and it was now 25 years later and Thomas had never met anyone to fall in Love with and spent his hours on his own making the Anatomical Heart in the hope that one day Claire would come into the Shop and see him. One Night while making the Anatomical Heart he realised that he created something very Beautiful and when the Anatomical Clock was finished he turned a small key on the side of Anatomical Heart and then Anatomical Heart started beating.

Thomas was over-joyed that his Anatomical Heart had worked as he had spent many Years making this Anatomical Heart that would mend his broken heart. Claire never did come back to Thomas little watch repair shop and every evening Thomas turned the key on the Anatomical Heart and use to watch it beating and then with tears in his eyes, he went to Bed on own. Thomas died in his Bed on his own and the people of Shillington Square where very sad that Thomas had died and everyone said how great Thomas was at fixing watches.

No-one took over Thomas Little Watch repair Shop and was left abandoned and time took it's toll on the Little Watch Repair Shop. Shillington Square went on about it's daily Business of market stalls and food shops of every kind.

So what happened to the Anatomical Heart I hear you ask?

The Anatomical Heart was sold at Auction after Thomas died and the Buyer of the Clock was Lady called Susan Doyle that had bought the Anatomical Heart as a Wedding Present for her Daughter who name was Claire.

Space-Truckin

Nicholas rocked in the Rocking Chair wearing the Nasa Space suit and dreamed of his New Adventures. Nicholas thought the Hot-Rod Car in the Service Station Garage looked like a lot of Fun. After Rocking in the Rocking Chair, Nicholas decided to get himself a Coke from the Coke machine and drank the Coke while looking at a Poster with the Nasa Space Shuttle on it.

Once Nicholas had drunk the Coke he put the Space Helmet Back onto the Suit and sung Elton John's Rocket Man while being inside the Spacesuit. Nicholas always saw himself as more of a Native American Indian sitting in a Teepee with a Indian Pipe, rather than an Astronaut flying through Space.

Nicholas decided to name the Hot-Rod in the Service Station Space-Truckin as it well with the theme of the Poster with the Space Shuttle. 52.4083 North, 1.5069 West

Helter Skelter Reprise
Written by Nicholas Robinson

3rd January 2014

I sat in the Hospital Bed in Wrexham General Hospital and thought about my next Adventures, I was being kept in Wrexham General Hospital for Observation and my vital signs where being monitored every hour. Mum had brought me some A4 paper and my coloured Pens so I could draw and also I had a Colouring Book that I like to Colour in. The Weather outside was quite bright and I enjoyed the rays of sun that where shining through the Hospital Ward Window.

Instead of drawing on the A4 paper I wrote down some New Idea's I had for more Adventures and my new Quest I was to set to work on. Soon it was time for the Nurse to check my vital signs again, the Nurse took my Blood Pressure and temperature and also measured how much oxygen was in my blood by putting a peg like device on my finger. After the Nurse took my Vital signs I then went back to creating more Adventures on the A4 piece of Paper. Over the last 4 years I have done some amazing Adventures and enjoyed so many different experiences and I was still writing New Adventures to go on. I have fell in love with idea of Going to Florida to experience the Water Slides and Theme Parks that are on offer in Orlando and to swim with Dolphins at Sea World, Discovery Cove. I eventually set to work and created a New drawing for my Next Adventures while sitting up in the Hospital Bed at Wrexham General Hospital.

9th January 2014

I spent the morning on New Brighton Promenade doing my Land Paddle-boarding that I have now fell in love with, the Longboard I chose for this Sport was a Dropdeck Atom Longboard for extra stability while I am paddling along the promenade. I noticed the Tide was coming in and I could see the waves crashing against the Perch Rock Light House and I paused for a moment on my Longboard and took in the Sea Air and gave myself a Warmful Smile.

11th January 2014

Me and Mum arrived at the Crocky Trail Farm just outside Chester for 8:30am, we had come to Crocky Trail for me to experience Hot Air Ballooning over the Cheshire Plains. We arrived at the Hot Air Balloon take off site, and found the Hot Air Balloon to be fully inflated. I met with the Pilot and my fellow Passengers that where having the Hot Air Balloon flight. After a short safety talk from the Balloon Pilot, we then got into the Hot Air Balloon Basket, which was quite a lot of room for all us passengers. The frost on the ground gave us all the indication that we where now in the Winter and this was going to be a very special flight in the Hot Air Balloon.

The Balloon took off and then the ground started to get smaller as we soared high above the Cheshire Plains in the Hot Air Balloon. What greeted me when the Balloon got high in the Sky was the Scenery becoming a Winter Wonderland as the Cheshire Plains was covered in a blanket of Snow and Ice. Flying in the Hot Air Balloon was very tranquil and exciting at the same time. When the Hot Air Balloon touched down about an hour later, the Pilot then opened a Bottle of Champagne and we toasted the Success of our Winter Wonderland Hot Air Balloon Flight.

The Garden of Aurora
Created by Nicholas Robinson/Drawings and writing by Nicholas Robinson

Prologue
Nicholas Robinson is an Adventurer and suffers from Mental Illness and is Autistic, Nicholas has spent the last 3 years doing incredible Adventures, Nicholas before he started his Adventures 2010 met the Great Clock that told Nicholas he would 3 years of amazing Adventures. The Adventures was called Nick's Adventures and was to end in Intensive Care Unit where Nicholas Died on his Birthday 28th May 2013 and Nicholas Became an Angel. In February 2013 and March 2013 Nicholas became very ill and had 2 overdoses and the Book of Nick's Adventures came to the attention of Health Professionals and the ending at New Brighton Beach and then Intensive Care unit, while Nicholas was ill in March 2013 he visited the Great Clock for second time.

The Second Meeting with The Great Clock, March 2013.

Nicholas, "My Adventures have been Beautiful, is it time for me to become an Angel".

The Great Clock "Your Adventures have been Beautiful, do not listen to Anyone on Earth all that the Book stands for must hold meaning".

Nicholas, "Can I redesign my Adventures, can I have more time?".

The Great Clock "You where never meant to go any further, the Book has to end, you have been given so much in 3 years.

Nicholas   "I would like to go to the Garden of Aurora

The Great Clock, "i will Grant You This one Request".

The Great Clock

Study Area Garden of Aurora

After talking to The Great Clock asking if I could go to the Garden of Aurora, I found myself sitting or more laying on the floor dressed in white tunic and white trousers.

I looked around me and saw that The Great Clock had granted me my wish and I was in the Garden of Aurora. To the left and right of me where two Water features which where very Beautiful, in the middle was a Window which read "Nick's Adventures". And in the Window was me in Intensive Care Unit, hooked up to various Medical Machines. This is what the Great Clock was showing me, this was the Ending to Nick's Adventures. To the left of the Window was a Fuzzle Funk Monkey a very Colourful Monkey and is very lovable. To the right of the Fuzzle Funk Monkey is a Goldfish Bowl and a writing Desk. I lay there on the Floor and in front of me was a Pen and a Large sheet of paper, I decided to write new Adventures and then I put a Question mark on the large piece of paper.

In front of me and the large piece of paper was the Time Key of Aurora the purpose of which is unknown to me. I decided I would explore the Garden as I wanted to spend time in the Garden of Aurora. I looked into the Window at me in Intensive Care Unit one more time and then went to look at other Gardens in the Garden of Aurora.

Study Area, Garden of Aurora

113

The Water Feature, Garden of Aurora

I had left the study Garden where there was a Window of me in Intensive Care Unit in a Hospital and now I was exploring the Garden of Aurora. The next area of the Garden of Aurora I came to was a Beautiful Water feature with Archimedes Screw to pump the water back to the top of the water feature. To the right of the Archimedes screw was a Sun Lounger and a massage pad with a colourful chequered Blanket with all different colours on it. I decided to sit on the Sun Lounger and watched the water feature and I was fascinated by watching the water being pumped back to the top of the water feature using an Archimedes screw. At the Bottom of the water feature. Where the fish was swimming enjoying the water being fed into the pond, creating fun and enjoyment for the fish.

In front of the water feature was Aurora Time Key, the time key had hour glass sand at it centre.

As I kept looking at the Water feature, I saw a little puzzle to the left of the water feature and the answer to the Puzzle was the word "Great" and sure enough I also found the word "Clock" at the top right of the Water feature. I decided to go and explore more of the Garden of Aurora. The Garden of Aurora is a very tranquil place and this water feature was very Beautiful.

Water Feature, Garden of Aurora

Crystal Glass Area, Garden of Aurora

The next part of the Garden of Aurora I came to was a pyramid style Glass Area with circular Mirrors going in different directions. To the right of the Pyramid and circular Mirrors was a stone table with the Time Key on it. While I stood looking at the Glass Pyramid something happened, the Sun was began to shine through the circular Mirrors and onto the Crystal Glass Pyramid, suddenly an array of Light and Colours shone in all different directions across the Crystal Glass Area. The Spectrum of Colour the Crystals Glass Pyramid was giving out was amazing. I sat by the Time Key on the stone table and watch the different Colours coming from the Glass Pyramid. I thought the coloured Glass Pyramid was Amazing, a truly Great Light Show. I concentrated on one circular Mirror at the left of the Glass Pyramid and something was written on the side of the Circular Mirror, it read "Great Clock". I was beginning to realise that Nick's Adventures was going to end, my Beautiful Adventures that have spanned 3 years is coming to end and the Garden of Aurora is my Sanctuary. I met the Great Clock 3 years ago and the Great Clock has given me Beautiful amazing Adventures and I have seen and done amazing things, and now i'm in the Garden of Aurora looking through a window at myself in Intensive Care Unit connected to a Ventilator and Medical Machines.

Crystal Glass Pyramid Area, Garden of Aurora

115

Glass Floor of Aurora, Garden of Aurora

I came across a Glass Floor while exploring the Garden of Aurora, above the Glass where Windows where I could see Space, Stars and Planets, one of the windows showed me The Great Clock waiting for my return to the Great Clock. Through the Glass Floor of Aurora I saw myself in Intensive Care Unit in Hospital. I stood there and watched myself in Intensive Care. I Watched Doctors and Nurses tending to me, suctioning my Lungs on the Ventilator, taking Blood samples, checking the machine settings. Doctors doing Medical tests on m, connecting EEG to look at my Brain activity, Nurses changing my Foley Catheter so I could urinate. Nurses changing a bag of milky liquid that I was hooked up to by an I.V Pole, the milky liquid went from the I.V Bag down a Red Tube through my Nose and went down my throat to my Stomach. The Endotracheal Tube that connects to the Ventilator also went down my throat and into my windpipe. There was a little Tube connected to the Endotracheal Tube that was used to inflate the Cuff of the Endotracheal Tube at the end of the Endotracheal Tube which was in the Windpipe. The Cuff on Endotracheal Tube is used to create an Airtight Airway for the Ventilator and stop anything else from entering the windpipe, while Endotracheal tube was in place, speech is impossible as Endotracheal Tube passes through the Vocal Chords.

I was connected to a lot of Medical Equipment, I stood and watched myself through the Glass Floor, I should have been sad but I was like in between, I was fascinated watching the Doctors and Nurses tending to me in there Surgical Scrubs while I lay there in Intensive Care Unit. I wondered what it would be like to Wake up on a Ventilator in Intensive Care, I couldn't decide whether that would be a Great Adventure or not, waking up in Intensive Care Unit Connected to all the Medical Equipment. The Intensive Care Unit was second to last Adventure in my Adventures, the last Adventure in my Book that I was following, I became an Angel and helped people on the way to Heaven.

Glass Floor of Aurora, Garden of Aurora

Music/Instrumental Area, Garden of Aurora

After looking at through the Glass Floor of Aurora seeing myself in an Intensive Care Unit, I decided to explore more of the Garden of Aurora. Shortly after going passed the Glass Floor of Aurora I found myself in a really cool Area a Musical Area with Guitars, a round Gong, Drums, a Beautiful Harp was at the centre of the Music Garden. There was an Amplifier and effect pedal for the Guitars and a speaker to the far right of the Music Garden, to the left of the Cong there was a Blue Hammer to hit the Cong with. To the left of the Blue Hammer was a wooden table with the Time Key of Aurora sitting on top of the Wooden Table. Above the Time Key of Aurora was a Fish tank and the background of the Tank was an ECG Trace, above the Drums on the right of the Garden was a island shore with Palm Trees and me laying on Sun Lounger watching the Sea.

In front of the Harp was a Medical Stethoscope which I picked up and had a listen to my Heart, the Heart is Lovely to listen to. The Guitars where Danelectro cool American Guitars, one Guitar was Semi-Acoustic Guitar called Danelectro Convertible, the other Guitar was a Electric Guitar which was a Danelectro DC-59

Psychedelic, which was multi coloured, I though this Guitar was far out.

I spent ages in the Music area of the Garden of Aurora, and I played all the Musical Instruments and I had lots of Fun and I enjoyed the Music/Instrumental Area of the Garden of Aurora. My favourite Music Instrument was Danelectro DC-59 Psychedelic

Music/Instrumental Area, Garden of Aurora

Sand Particle Garden, Garden of Aurora

I had really enjoyed the Musical Instrumental Area of the Garden of Aurora and wondered what the next Garden was, the next was created with Sand, it was very stunning, to the left the Sand Garden there was a Umbrella Fountain with different coloured water drops. There was two like swan Birds with Pink Beaks, next to the Multi-Coloured Umbrella Fountain was a Chair and foot stool, behind the Chair was a half circle Water feature with at the Bottom was a pond. To the right of the Chair was a Beehive with lots of Bees circling around the Beehive, to the right of the Beehive was a Water-feature. To the centre behind the Multi-Coloured Umbrella Fountain was cascading Sand Feature, the sand feature used a

Rack to push the Sand down the sand Waterfall, the floor of this Garden was all Sand. The Time Key of Aurora was sunken in the Water below the Multi-Coloured Umbrella Fountain. In the Sand Particle Garden there was four flying Butterflies with different coloured wings. I sat in the Chair and put my feet on the foot stool and enjoyed the Sand Particle Garden. I loved all the Animals in this Garden, this a really Tranquil Area of the Garden of Aurora. I watched the Multi-Coloured Umbrella Fountain and enjoyed watching all the Colours, and listening to the Bee's going about there Business. In the Sky the Sun was shining and the Sand cascading down the Sand Feature, Sand Particle Garden was very Beautiful.

Sand Particle Area, Garden of Aurora

Falling Wall of Aurora, Garden of Aurora

I was exploring more of the Garden of Aurora when I came across a Brick Red Wall, to the left of the Brick Red was a White Handle and a Blue leaf Branch on the Floor by the Red Brick Wall. As I was trying to think where to explore next in the Garden of Aurora. Suddenly the Red Brick Wall started moving inwards on it's itself creating a vacuum into Space. I dived for the Blue leaf Branch and

119

hung onto it, the force of the vacuum was great. I looked to see where the Red Brick Wall once stood was now Space and in the Distance was the Great Clock pulling me towards it.

I hung onto the Blue Leaf Branch with all my strength I could muster but I found myself slipping towards the vacuum of Space and towards the Great Clock. I decided to attempt to push the White handle and see where that led me, I was really frightened, I didn't want to get sucked into Space and back to the Great Clock. I pushed the White Handle and used all my Strength and made my way through the Secret Entrance that Red Brick Wall Had Hidden. I had been crying a lot while holding onto the Blue leaf Branch and my face was streaming with tears. After using all my strength to push open the secret door of the Red Brick Wall, I now found myself in a Secret Garden with lots of flowers and a Hot-tub.

Falling Wall of Aurora, Garden of Aurora

Secret Garden of Aurora, Garden of Aurora

I had finally made it passed the Falling Wall of Aurora and now I found myself in a Secret Garden with Beautiful Flowers and a Hot Tub. I decided that I would have nice soak in the Hot Tub and then look at my surrounding of the secret Garden from the Hot Tub. I took my clothes off and got into the Hot Tub to enjoy a nice soak. While in the Hot Tub I looked at the Secret Garden, to the left of the Hot Tub was the Secret Entrance to Red Brick Wall, to the right of the Falling Wall Secret entrance was a lever to De-activate the Falling Wall of Aurora, in front of me was a Statue of me as an Angel, in front of the Statue was a Water slide that went back to the Garden of Aurora. If I wanted to go back to the Garden of Aurora/main Garden I would have to turn the Statue of myself as an Angel to activate the Water for the slide to go back to the Main Garden. To the left of the waterslide was a Blue Leaf Tree, and a notice that said " Climb the Blue Leaf Tree for Fun".
I sat in the Hot Tub and drunk a mug of Coffee from a small round table and decided I wanted to climb the Blue Leaf Tree for Fun. I got out the Hot Tub after I had a nice soak and I got changed and then I made my over to the Blue Leaf Tree and started climbing, the Tree was very Big and it was a long climb and I enjoyed climbing the Tree and seeing the Blue Leaves.

Secret Garden of Aurora, Garden of Aurora

Sherbet of Aurora, Garden of Aurora

I finally got to the end of climbing the Blue Leaf Tree and found myself looking at a landing pad with a Gyrocopter named Sherbet, around me was Giant sweet Sherbet tubes with Liquorice.

I could see Sun shining down on me, to the right of me was mock up controls for the Gyrocopter. I decided to practice with the mock-up controls before flying the Gyrocopter. I practiced with the controls on the mock-up simulator then finally I was ready to fly the Gyrocopter Sherbet.

I made my way to the Red Gyrocopter and climbed into the cockpit and strapped myself in, then I pressed the engine switch on Button. Suddenly the engine came alive and made aloud noise. Gyrocopter had come to life with the push of button, the blades of the Gyrocopter started to rotate, then when I was ready I pushed the Lever for the Gyrocopter to fly forwards. I was now flying above the skies of the Garden of Aurora. It took me a while to get to fly Sherbet the Gyrocopter and I was really having a lot of fun flying doing turns and doing stunts with the Gyrocopter seeing Aurora from the Air was a Great sight. I felt the strength of the wind through my Crash Helmet visor as the Gyrocopter was pushing through the Air.

Sherbet of Aurora, Garden of Aurora

Meeting of Felldoran The Dragon, Sky of Aurora

Felldoran: "Hi Nicholas, I'm Felldoran the Dragon

Nicholas: " Are you the Dragon that has been chasing me for last two weeks, and can me to see me while I was in Hospital on 3rd March 2013.

Felldoran: "Yes, Nicholas. It was me who put the tree of Fun in the Secret Garden, so you would find Sherbert the Gyrocopter when you climbed the Tree of Fun.

Nicholas: " I want to alter the Ending to my Adventures that I have started in February 2010 and end on 28th May 2013, where I become an Angel".

Felldoran: " It is within my Power for your Adventures to continue and ending can be altered, follow the path to the Cave of Imagaination, there you will find the Heart of the Great Clock, but beware that you may not like what you find at the Heart of the Great Clock. I have used my Dragon Magic so you can still do your Adventures beyond May 2013.

Nicholas: " Thankyou Felldoran The Dragon".

Natural Spring of Aurora, Garden of Aurora

After meeting Felldoran The Dragon above the Sky of Aurora I was very Happy within myself while flying above the skies of Aurora I saw a landing pad to land Sherbert the Gyrocopter.

I landed on the landing pad and climbed out of the Gyrocopter and found myself at the Natural spring of Aurora. The Spring was Giant Tap and I had to turn handle of the large Tap for the natural spring water. On front of the large tap was a Table with a Buffet Spread with lots of food for me to eat. At the Natural Spring the Windows where views od Outer Space, I looked at Planets and stars, and a Comet. There was a Chair by the Buffet table and I sat down and started to eat from the Buffet. I was really Happy that I had met Felldoran The Dragon and Felldoran the Dragon had granted me an extension on my Adventures. My New Adventures would be Chronicles and would start on 25th May 2013 in Year of Red Knight. My New Adventures would be "The Chronicles of Nicholas The Red". I was really excited as I sat eating the Buffet at the Natural Spring of the Garden of Aurora. I had enjoyed flying Sherbert the Gyrocopter and all the other Area's of the Garden of Aurora I have so far explored.

Natural Spring of Aurora, Garden of Aurora

Teepee of Aurora, Garden of

After the Buffet in the Natural Spring Garden of Aurora, I once again starting to explore the Garden of Aurora, I followed a path with a sign saying "this way to Teepee of Aurora".
After following the path I came across a North American Teepee with a Felldoran the Dragon Totem Pole. To the of the Teepee was a sign saying " Great Spa of Aurora this Way". Next to the sign was an Indian style Canoe, I guessed I was going to have to paddle the Indian Canoe over to the Great Spa of Aurora across the water. Across the water lay the Great Spa of Aurora, the Spa was like Mayan Pyramids and the Spa looked stunning. In front of the Teepee was a Northern American Headdress on aa stone body sculpture on the bottom of the stone sculpture it read " path to the Sun is across the Water". I assumed the sign was about getting to the Great Spa of Aurora of Aurora.
I decided to climb into the Teepee and have some Fun, I found a Peace Pipe and I decided to have a few Puffs of the Indian Peace Pipe and then went to the Entrance of the Teepee and sat there looking across the Water to the Great Spa of Aurora. I decided I would paddle the Indian Canoe across the Lake and visit the Great Spa of Aurora. I made my way to the Canoe and pushed the Canoe off the shore and got into the Canoe and started paddling the Indian Canoe across the Lake to the Great Spa of Aurora.

Teepee of Aurora, Garden of Aurora

125

Gateway to Intensive Care Maze, Garden of Aurora

I was half way paddling the Indian Canoe across the lake to get to the Great Spa, when suddenly i heard a large Thunder sound and the Sky went Dark. The Sun was shining Bright and had now been eclipsed by a Black Moon. A tear in the sky appeared showing Outer Space and the Great Clock with it causeway. It was now Raining fiercely with heavy Thunder and fork Lightning. I was soaked to the skin paddling the Indian Canoe as fast as I could to get out of the Storm and away from the Great Clock. The Heavy Rain kept coming down Heavier and Heavier, the Lightning became even more fierce. The Sun had completely Gone, suddenly as I was paddling through the Storm created by The Great Clock , a whirl Pool formed on the Lake and Myself and the Indian Canoe started swirling around the whirlpool the Great Clock had Created. At the Bottom of the Whirlpool was a Black Hole, as I was swirling around the Waves from the Lake rolled over me and Broke up my Indian Canoe and then I fell through the Blackhole. The Great Clock had made this Storm on the Lake. I fell through the Black Hole into the Darkness. I kept falling and falling only seeing Blackness as there was nothing else. I thought Felldoran The Dragon had used his Magic to extend my Adventures. Now the Great Clock had sent me falling down a Black Hole.

Gateway to Intensive Care Maze, Garden of Aurora

The Great Clock Vs Felldoran The Dragon

Felldoran: " Leave Nicholas alone, I have extended his Adventures, Nicholas has nothing to do with you".

The Great Clock: " Nicholas must complete his Adventures that End in May 2013, I have gave Nicholas so much joy in the last three years. Nicholas be having a Beautiful Ending, he has had amazing Adventures but it time for him to become Angel and help People go to Heaven.

Felldoran: " I have used my Magic to extend his Adventures, Nicholas loves doing his Adventures, trapping Nicholas in the Intensive Care Unit Maze won't work. Nicholas will find away out of the Intensive Care Maze.

The Great Clock: " So What!, if he does find away out of the Intensive Care Maze, you can't use your Magic forever, I Know That. Your Magic is not as strong as mine, Nicholas will come back to me".

Felldoran the Dragon: " My Magic and Power is as Strong as yours I am Felldoran The Dragon, I will help Nicholas".

The Great Clock Vs Felldoran The Dragon

Intensive Care Maze, The Great Clock

After I went through the Black Hole I fell and hit the Ground and I Hurt my Arm falling through the Blackhole. I looked around to see where I was, I was in a maze with windows of me in Intensive care Unit in Hospital. The Windows showed me different angles of me in Intensive Care unit, the Maze was over-whelming to me, seeing myself in all the Windows in Intensive Care Unit was too much for me. I started to cry and I could only manage one tear. I decided I would try and find my way out of the Intensive care Maze. I tried different routes through the Intensive Care Maze, but I kept getting lost through the Maze, I thought was never going to find my way out of the Intensive Care Maze. Then I saw in some Windows the Time Key of Aurora, I thought to myself I f I follows the Mirrors with the time Key of Aurora in them, I might find my way out of the Maze. I tried following the Windows with the Time Key of Aurora and found that I started to get somewhere. The images of me Intensive care Unit didn't bother me anymore, seeing images of me in Intensive Care at first shocked me. I followed the Mirrors with the Time Key of Aurora and eventually found the exit to the Intensive Care Unit Maze, I was glad I was out the Maze.

Intensive Care Unit Maze, The Great Clock

The Great Spa of Aurora, Garden of Aurora

Finally I was out of the Intensive Care Maze that the Great Clock had put me in, in front of me when I existed the Maze was three steps and a Lady with Pink Dress and a Colourful Headdress on.

The Lady put Flowers around my neck and said to me "Welcome to the Great Spa of Aurora, Nicholas". The Spa was like Mayan Pyramid with Colourful Flowers all around, by the Entrance to the Great Spa of Aurora was Butterflies flying around. In front of the Entrance to the Great Spa was two Women to Greet me again to the Great Spa. To the right of the two Women by the Entrance to the Great Spa was a colourful Headdress, the colours on this Headdress was amazing.

I made my way to the Entrance to the Great Spa entrance, and the two women at the entrance put the colourful Headdress on my head, and once again I was welcomed to the Great Spa of Aurora.

The two women made sure I was ready to go into the entrance of the Great Spa, I was given a Glow Torch, and women explained that I had to follow the Stones across the Pond, this Entrance to the Great Spa was called the Butterfly Entrance. After being made a fuss of by the three ladies at the Entrance of the Great Spa, I took a deep Breathe and made my way into the Butterfly Entrance to the Great Spa of Aurora. I left behind the Intensive Care Maze which I didn't like, ahead of me lay the Beautiful Spa of Aurora.

The Great Spa of Aurora, Garden of Aurora

129

Nicholas Robinson

Butterfly Entrance to Great Spa of Aurora

I walked through the Entrance of the Great Spa of Aurora, I had my way out of the Intensive care maze, and i had gone through the welcoming Ladies who gave me flower necklace and colourful headdress. The Entrance I was told by the three women was called the Butterfly Entrance, and the three ladies explained to me that the Reception for the Great Spa was through the Butterfly Entrance. I found out why it was called the Butterfly Entrance to the Great Spa. There was lots of Butterflies around me, all the butterflies where different colours and it was a very Beautiful place to be. On the floor of the Butterfly Entrance was pure Blue Water with stepping stones for me to make my way to the Reception of Great Spa of Aurora. I made my way across the stepping Stones with the Glow Torch the ladies had given me outside the Butterfly Entrance. I thought the Butterflies where Beautiful, there colours where amazing, as well as the Butterflies there was spotlights with Yellow and Orange Rays admitting from the Water. I made my way along the Stepping stones watching the colourful Butterflies. I loved being in this entrance with all the Butterflies circling around me, and I loved my colourful Headdress the women outside the Butterfly Entrance had given me. Soon I came to the Reception of the Great Spa of Aurora. I had enjoyed the experience of the Butterfly Entrance.

Butterfly Entrance to Great Spa of Aurora
130

Reception for the Great Spa of Aurora

I got to the Reception of the Great Spa of Aurora, and just finished going through the Beautiful Butterfly Entrance. I was welcomed by a Lady with a warm smile behind a reception Desk. The Lady told me her name was Sophie and could I please take a seat and the Nurse will be with you shortly, while I waited on the Couch in the Reception, Sophie brought a Coffee for me and Biscuits and welcomed me to the Great Spa of Aurora. On the Wall next to the couch I was sitting was a Beautiful Mosaic Picture. I sat and relaxed and drunk and I ate the Biscuits.

After I had the coffee and Biscuits, I then sat there waiting for the Nurse. Then a Nurse came from around the Reception Desk and greeted me. The Nurse was wearing a Red Mandarin Collared Nurses Dress with a White Belt, Flowery Arm Cuffs and colourful Headdress. The Nurse told me her name was Nurse Maria Thorton and was one of the Nurses at the Great Spa of Aurora.

Nurse Thorton told me before I can enter the Great Spa of Aurora I needed to have a Medical done by a lovely lady Doctor, the lady doctor name was Dr Shakari and Dr Shakari would be doing my Medical in the Exam Room. After the Medical I would be taken to another waiting area, as the Doctor decided a treatment plan while I was at the Great Spa of Aurora. The Nurse told me to relax through the Medical and the Nurse told me enjoy the Great Spa of Aurora as the treatments at the Spa where very Blissful and relaxing.

Reception for Great Spa of Aurora

The Medical for the Great Spa of Aurora

I followed Nurse Thorton into the Exam room, the Doctor was already waiting for me in the Exam Room ready to give me the Medical. The Doctor had Brown Hair with Highlights with Yellow flower in her Hair. The Doctor was wearing Pink Surgical Scrubs, over the pink surgical scrubs the Doctor was wearing a Red Lab Coat, the Lady Doctor looked stunning so did Nurse Maria Thorton is her Nurses Uniform. The Doctor greeted me in the exam room, and told me her name was Doctor Shakari and she would be doing the Medical with Nurse Thorton. The Nurse told me to remove my White tunic and white waist belt and to sit on the Medical Bed. I did as requested and removed my top and sat on the Medical Bed. The Nurse again told me to relax through the Medical as I was getting excited. The Doctor and Nurse Thorton started the Medical, the Doctor looked my ears, shone a light in my eyes, looked in my mouth, felt for lumps on my neck, took my pulse at the wrist and neck. Then Dr Shakari tested my reflexes at the Knee and elbow. Then I was asked to lay on the Medical Bed and told to Cough to make sure everything below was alright. Then the Nurse took my Weight and Height. Then Dr Shakari and Nurse Thorton told me that the first part of the Medical was finished and i was going to have an MRI scan of my Brain and a Chest X-ray. Nurse Thorton and the Doctor took me to the MRI Machine and I lay on down and MRI scan took a while and then after the MRI scan, I had a Chest x-ray. After both MRI and Chest X-ray was done, Nurse Thorton took me back to the Exam room for the Third part of the Medical at the Great Spa of Aurora. The Nurse told me to sit back on the Medical Bed in the Exam room, the Nurse told me again to relax as the Doctor would be looking at my Heart Rhythm. Nurse Thorton then put a Blood pressure cuff around my Arm and put a oxygen Blood peg on one of my fingers to see how much oxygen was in my Blood. The Nurse took my Blood pressure and Cuff went tight against my upper arm. After taking my Blood pressure the Nurse took a Thermometer and put it in my left Ear and took my Temperature. Once the Nurse had taken my Temperature, the Nurse told me there would be sharp scratch and the Nurse inserted a Butterfly Cannula to get a Blood Samples from me. The Butterfly Cannula was left in my Arm in case they needed more Blood Samples. After these tests the to listened to my chest with Stethoscope and asked me lay down on the Medical Bed to Listen to my stomach. After the Doctor had finished listening to my chest and stomach, I was asked to blow into a lung function Machine to test my Lungs. After the Lung function test I was wired up by the

Nurse to a 12 lead ECG and 3 Lead ECG Machines. Once again Nurse Thorton told me to relax as they where listening to my Heart. I looked down at myself on the Medical Bed and saw wires and tubes all over me, I was very wired up. The Doctor took the ECG Readings and then I was disconnected from the ECG Machines. After ECG the Doctor did an Eye Sight test, the Nurse had the Chest X-ray and MRI scan of my Brain and put both pictures on light board. After the eye sight test, the last part of the Medical I had go to the toilet and use a sample bottle to get a Urine Sample. After going to the Toilet, I was led back into the exam room. I was asked to sit on the Medical Bed by the Doctor. Then the Doctor explained that she would be putting a treatment plan together for me, and the Doctor told me that Nurse Thorton would take me to a waiting area called the Pond of the Beautiful Dragonflies, there I was to relax and unwind watching the Dragonflies while Doctor Shakari put my treatment plan in place at Great Spa of Aurora. Then after the Doctor had talked to me the Nurse helped me put my White Tunic back on and white waist belt back on and then took me by the hand and took me to the waiting area of the Pond of the Beautiful Dragonflies.

Medical for The Great Spa of Aurora.
With MRI Scan Picture, Chest X-ray, 12 lead ECG, 3 Lead ECG, blood Pressure Cuff, Oxygen Blood Peg, Lung Function Machine, Heart Anatomy   Picture.Height and Weight Scales.

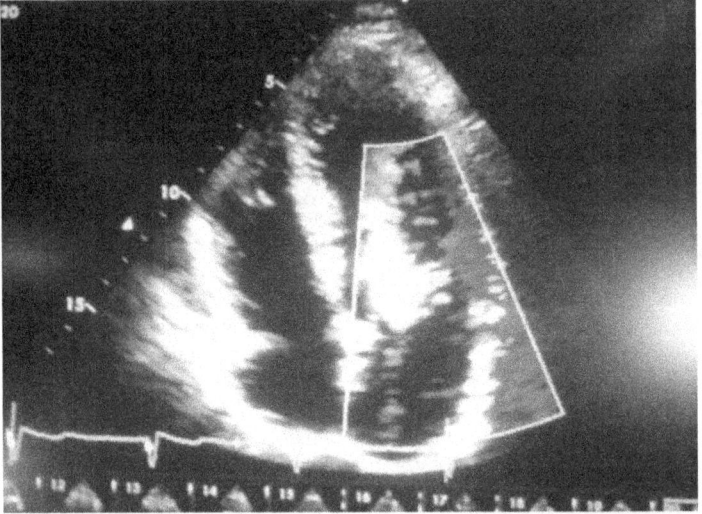

Nicholas Robinson Heart, taken from Echo-Cardiogram, Heart Ultrasound.
John Moores University, Cardio Suite Research, Liverpool
11/3/2013

Pond of Beautiful Dragonflies, The Great Spa of Aurora

I followed Nurse Thorton down a series of corridors and then we came into a Garden where there was a Sun Lounger type Bed a Beautiful Mayan Rug on the floor, to the right of the rug was a swim ladder. I thought about going for a swim, next to the Sun Lounger was white table with a Jug of Water and a cup. Also on the White table was a small vase with Yellow Flowers. Then I saw all the Yellow Dragonflies, it was amazing to watch against the Blue Water. I stood next to Nurse Thorton and watched the Yellow Dragonflies, I couldn't take my eyes of the Yellow Dragonflies. Nurse Thorton told me to lay on the Lounger and she would fetch a Orange Blanket and a pillow for me.

I lay on the Sun Lounger and then Nurse Thortonn came back with a Blanket and pillow, Nurse lay the blanket over me and told me that the blanket was to keep me warm. Then Nurse fluffed up the Pillow and put it behind my head. Nurse Thorton again told me to Relax as I was getting excited watching the Yellow Dragonflies.

134

The Nurse told me she would be back shortly for me to take me to Doctor Shakari Consultant Room for by Treatment Plan at the Great Spa of Aurora. Nurse before she left made sure I was snuggled up in the Sun Lounger and then went back out the Garden. I lay there on the Sun Lounger and watched the Beautiful Yellow Dragonflies all around me. I was very relaxed after watching the Yellow Dragonflies, I fell in love with the Pond of Beautiful Dragonflies.

I had a cup of water, and taste of the water was amazing. After watching the Yellow Dragonflies I went to Sleep in this Blissful Garden.

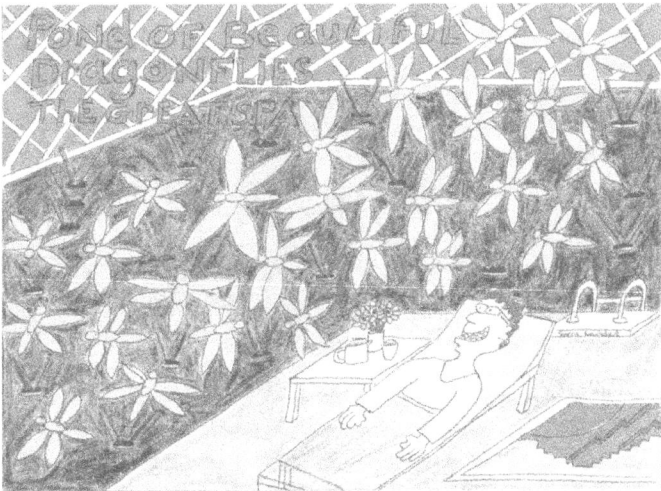

Pond of the Beautiful Dragonflies, Great Spa of Aurora

Consultation Room, Dr Shakari, Great Spa of Aurora

I was fast a sleep in the Sun Lounger by the Pond of the Beautiful Dragonflies when Nurse Thorton woke me up. Nurse Thorton told me that the Doctor would see me in her consultation room about my Treatment plan at the Great Spa of Aurora. I got up from the Lounger at Beautiful Dragonfly Garden and then Nurse Thorton led me by the hand to Dr Shakari office. On the way to the consultation room Nurse Thorton noticed, I was getting nervous and the Nurse told me to relax and she would be in consultation room as well and that Dr Shakari is a Lovely Doctor. We got to consultation room and Nurse Thorton opened the door, and I was greeted by the doctor Shakari sitting behind her desk. The Doctor told me I needed to have a lot of colour and my first treatment would be Tantric Therapy which I had never heard of before. The Doctor had also included a Sleep Study, V-max fitness test, Cardio Test and Echo-cardiogram ultrasound of the Heart. Doctor Shakari told me that they wanted to make sure that my Heart was still Lovely and Kind. The Doctor talked to me for about an Hour and I would be receiving a lot of treatment. After the consultation Nurse Thorton told me I would be prepared for my first treatment, Nurse Thorton then led me by the Hand and then we went out of Dr Shakari Office to the Preparation room for my stay at the Great Spa of Aurora.

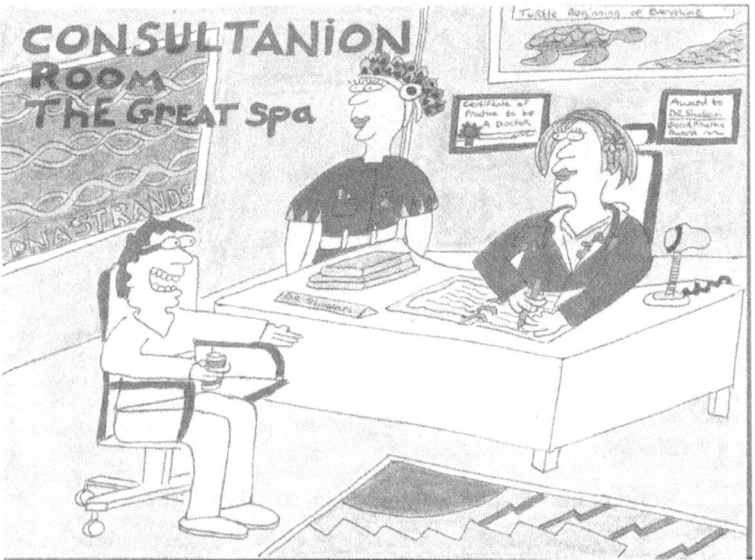

Consultation Room, Dr Shakari, Nicholas Treatment Plan, Spa of Aurora

Dr Shakari Medical Report

Spa Guest/Patient: Nicholas Robinson Date of Birth 28/5/1977 Height 6ft, Weight 13.5 stone

After carrying out extensive Medical Exam on Nicholas I have found Nicholas to have a lack of Colour and is very White and Nicholas looks very sad even through his Lovely smile. Nicholas Blood Pressure was fine and Blood work came back with good results. MRI scan and Chest x-ray where fine. I will be including a Sleep Study and V-max fitness test, Cardio tilt test and Echo-Cardiogram as I would like to make sure Nicholas Heart Beats with Love and Kindness.

I have have put Trantric Therapy for Nicholas as his first treatment at the Spa to bring back the Colour into Nicholas. I have included Nicholas to have extensive treatments at the Spa to make a full recovery from his sadness. After all the treatments are done and I am Happy with Nicholas Wellbeing then Nicholas can become Nicholas the Red and go back to the Garden of Aurora.

Dr Shakari, Consultatnt, Great Spa of Aurora

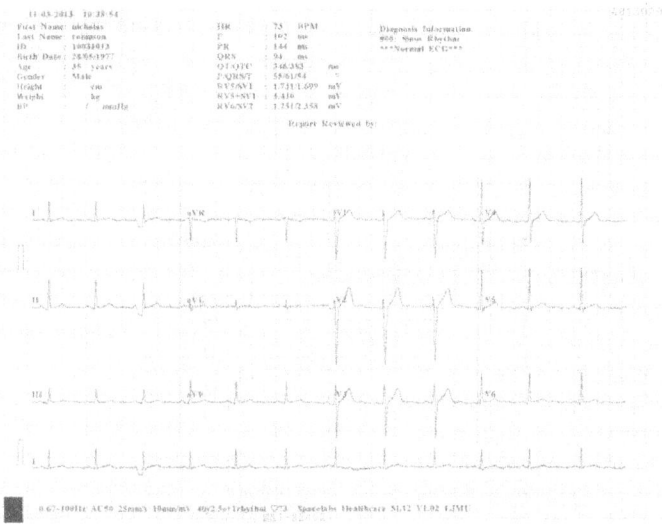

Nicholas Robinson ECG Trace, Cardio Suite, John Moores University, Liverpool 11/3/2013

Preparation Area to Enter Great Spa of Aurora

Nurse Thorton lead me by the Hand from the consultation room to the preparation room. We got to the preparation room door and I opened the Door and saw it was like a bathroom and straight ahead of me was Red and Pink Surgical Scrubs, Pink pair of Crocs plastic shoes, and Pink like dressing Gown and a Yellow necklace and Yellow flower to clip into my hair. The Nurse told me use the Shower cubicle to get changed and put around myself as I would be having a nice hot bath. I did as I was instructed and went into shower cubicle and took all my clothes off and put a towel around my waist. I got out of the shower cubicle and the Bath was ready for me, the Nurse told me to get in the Bath and she would Bath me, I told Nurse Thorton I had never had a women bath me before, Nurse Thorton was not listening to me. In a Clinical way Nurse Thorton Bathed me and made sure I was clean, then the Nurse asked me to step out of the Bath then she dried me off with a Towel, then I was instructed to sit on the Bench while the Nurse prepared the Shaving Kit to shave my Face.

Once again Nurse Thorton in a Professional Manner Shaved my face, after the Shave Nurse Thorton told me to wash my Teeth using a medium Toothbrush and use the other side of the toothbrush to clean my tongue. Once Nurse Thorton was satisfied that I was clean. She decided that it was time for me to put on the new clothes as I would no longer needing the White Tunic or White Trousers any more. I was helped by the Nurse to put on the New Clothes, after Nurse Thorton had helped me put on the Red and Pink Surgical Scrubs and the Pink Croc plastic shoes, and the Pink Robe with the Red Belt. After I put my Robe on the Nurse then put the flower Necklace around my Neck and to finish Nurse Thorton put a Yellow Flower into my Red Hair. After I finished putting on my new clothes on Nurse Thorton told me to look in the Mirror by the Sink, I went to the Mirror and looked at myself I noticed I had White Skin and I told the Nurse I was upset to see this. Nurse Thorton told me that why Dr Shakari had chosen Tantra Therapy for my first treatment to bring back the Colour into me. I had lots of Questions to ask Nurse Thorton about my Treatments, I was told once again to relax and enjoy the Treatments. Nurse Thorton decided I was ready to have my first treatment and my Therapist name was Alisha and she would be taken me for my Tantra Therapy Treatment.

Nurse Thorton opened the Door of preparation room and led by the hand to the Tantra Therapy Suite, I was relaxed and excited at the same time, Nurse Thorton was smiling as well.

Tantra Therapy, Great Spa of Aurora

Nurse Thorton and I arrived at the Tantra Therapy Suite and Norse Thorton told me to take a seat on the bench. Then as I sat on the Bench the Nurse told me she was going to Alisha in Tantra Therapy room about my Treatment. As I sat on the Bench in Tantra Therapy Suite I took stock at my surroundings and saw a ten armed statue which I thought was amazing and an indian circle ornament on the wall, the Tantra Therapy suite was a Beautiful area. After looking at the statue the door of Tantra Therapy Room Opened and Nurse Thorton and Therapist Alisha walked into the Tantra Therapy suite. The Therapist Alisha Greeted me and asked how I was feeling, I told alisha I was very sad and my skin was White and I love to smile and be happy. Nurse Thorton standing next to Therapist Alisha told me that she would leave me in the capable hands of Alisha and I would see Nurse Thorton later on. The Therapist Alisha sat on the Bench next to me and we talked about why I was sad about my Adventures, how I would like new Adventures, and be happy again. Alisha told in the next couple of Hours we together would explore my Adventures and bring back my happiness and my Love of Colour. I followed Therapist Alisha into the Tantra Therapy Room, the Tantra Therapy room was very soothing with massage table in the middle of the room and cabinet as well, pink wall with low soothing relaxing music. The Therapist told me that she would leave the room while I undressed and I was to lay on the table covered up with the large towel that was on the

139

massage table. Alisha left the room and I did what Alisha told me to do and lay on the massage table covered up by the large towel. After a couple of Minutes Alisha knocked on the Door and asked if I was ready, I replied I was and then Alisha walked in with a smile and told me that she would now start the Therapy. Alisha started giving me a scalp massage and told me I had a lot of tension built up and she would help me relax, after a couple of minutes having a scalp massage I was in a blissful relaxed state. After the scalp massage Alisha lit Sum candles around the room and then told me to lay on my side covered up. Alisha told me that she wanted me to go into a deep relaxed state, and the next part of the Therapy would bring the Colour back into me. Within 10 minutes of the Tantra Therapy Alisha had me in Deep relaxed state, I was very Happy and Blissful, feeling very content and I felt loving Harmony all around me.

Tantra Therapy Suite, Great Spa of Aurora

Dreaming Room, The Great Spa of Aurora

I lay there in Tantra Therapy room in a Deep relaxing state when suddenly I heard a noise telling me to wake up. I opened my eyes to Alisha looking down at me, Alisha told me that the Body and Mind must be in Equilibrium balanced together and I had been given deep relaxation in this treatment.

Alisha told she would leave the room and I would get dressed and sit on the massage table and then I would be taken to the Dream Room to a lovely Relaxing sleep. I got dressed and sat on the massage bed and then Alisha knocked on the Door and asked alright to come in, I said yes I am ready for the dream room. Alisha walked into the Therapy room with a Glass of Ice lemon for me to take with me to the Dream Room, Alisha helped me of the Bed and took me by the hand to the Dream Room. Alisha had to help as I was still virtual a sleep and not steady on my feet. We got to the Dream room and I lay on a Special made Bed on the floor and watched Beautiful colours on the ceiling, Alisha put my Glass of Ice Lemon on a small table next to the Bed and I went into a deep, and dreamed about new adventures and being Happy and my heart feeling the warmth of Joy and Love. I had enjoyed my first treatment at the Great Spa of Aurora, and now I was in Blissful sleep in the beautiful Dream Room,"Dreaming of Adventures". I fell a sleep in the Dream Room, feeling very relaxed in blissful state. I fell in a sleep and started dreaming in the Beautiful Dream room.
I had two dreams in the Dream Room, the first dream I found myself as a Flower in a large plant pot filled with soil, in my hand where to giant leafs, around my face I could feel a weight, I looked like a beautiful Flower. There was two ladies in the Dream and very looked they where from Movie Stepford Wives. They had nice dresses on and hats one the Women had watering cans in Her Hand, and then the lady with water can poured water into the plant pot and I start Automatically started dancing. The Second Dream I had in the Dream Room was very cool, I was an Hawaii Beach with an Orange and White Campervan, I had a Barbeque going, I had a Dark purple robe on, I had a Guitar on the Beach. I had a Surfboard so I could go Surfing. I sat in the Chair next to the Campervan and enjoyed the Barbeque, that after watching the Ocean, I went surfing in the waves and going inside the Waves and caught my first tube (going into the barrel of the Wave), then in the evening I watched the Sun go Down and then I went into the Orange and White Campervan and went to sleep. Then I woke up in the Dream Room in Great Spa of Aurora.

Dream Room, First Dream. Spa of Aurora

Dream Room, Second Dream, Spa of Aurora

Dining Area of the Great Spa of Aurora

After experiencing the Dream room and Tantric Therapy, Alisha took me to the Dining Area of the Spa, the food was laid out like a Buffet. I took a plate and got some Chicken drumsticks and sat at the Glass window of the spa of Aurora. Alisha told me there was a couple of hours before the next Therapy and if I felt like it take the elevator to the treetop canopy to see the colourful Parrots, Alisha told me that the Elevator was situated in the wet area of the Great Spa of Aurora, come out of the Dining area and follow the signs to the wet area of the Great Spa of Aurora. I sat there eating the food and looking out the Window, the Sun was shining and it was very Beautiful to watch while I ate. I sat at the table in the dining area and I reflexed about my Journey I had been through in the Garden of Aurora. I had flown a Gyrocopter, played a Guitar in Music Garden, seen amazing Gardens, I was nearly sucked into space at the falling wall, I found my way out of the Intensive care unit Maze. I had met Felldoran the Dragon above the Skies of Aurora. I am now at the Great Spa of Aurora, had a Medical at the Spa by Dr Shakari and I am now having treatments at the Great Spa of Aurora. I wondered what the Treetop Canopy was going to be like, I decided I would take a look at the Treetop Canopy.

Dining Area, Great Spa of Aurora

Treetop Canopy, Great Spa of Aurora

I finished eating in Dining area of the Great Spa of Aurora, and then I got up and followed the signs to wet area of the Great Spa. I followed the signs and soon I came across the wet area of the Spa of Aurora. The wet area was amazing there was a 50 metre swimming pool which I could swim in, a diving pool and lots of different water slides. There was a rapid River where you floated around, an outdoor swimming pool with Waterslides, there was a steam room and sauna with a cold plunge pool. I saw the elevator and I got into the Elevator and pressed the button for the Treetop canopy. I arrived at the Treetop Canopy and I looked through the Glass of the Elevator and I saw all the colourful Birds and lush Greenery of the Treetop Canopy. I stepped out of the elevator and stood there looking at all the Birds and Animals, the Colourful Parrots where amazing so where all the other Birds, there where colourful Lizards of all different colours. To the left of the Elevator was a desk and a Chair and to the Right was a Bed Lounger. In front of me was a Yellow Waterslide that went back to the Great Spa of Aurora. I spent hours in the Treetop Canopy it was a very Beautiful place to be. I used the desk to Write New Adventures and I listened to the noises of the birds and animals. I was over-whelmed by the colour of the Birds and animals. Being surrounded by colour I started writing new adventures and I wrote lots of new Adventures to do, I had fell in love with treetop canopy of the Great of Aurora.

Treetop Canopy, Great Spa of Aurora

Waterslide Back to the Spa of Aurora

After spending many hours in the Treetop Canopy I decided to use the Waterslide to get back to the wet area of the Great Spa of Aurora.it occurred to me how would I get my clothes back down to the wet area, as I had come to the treetop canopy fully clothed. I had swim shorts on but what about my robe and pink surgical scrubs. I put my clothes in the elevator and pressed the button for the elevator to go down with my clothes and a towel for me. After putting my clothes in the elevator I made my way to the waterslide, and I pushed myself down the Yellow Waterslide. The waterslide was amazing it was very long with tight turns and huge drops and I was going at very fast speed. The waterslide went around in circles on itself. Eventually I came out of the Waterslide and found myself back in the Wet Area of the Garden of Aurora. I got out of the Waterslide and my way to the Elevator to collect my clothes and the Towel. After collecting my clothes and towel from the elevator I went to the changing area and got changed and put my Pink Surgical Scrubs on and Pink Robe and pink croc plastic shoes and then I followed the signs back to the Dining Area of the Spa.

In the Dining Area I got a Glass of Orange Juice and sat down and looked out the Window looking at the Garden of Aurora. I was starting to wonder what my next therapy would be at the Great Spa of Aurora, I finished my Orange Juice and waited.

Waterslide Back to The Great Spa of Aurora

145

Yoga & Meditation, Great Spa of Aurora

I sat in the Dining area of the Spa and was watching the Sun shining on the Garden Aurora, when a lovely Lady stepped in front of me and greeted me, the lovely name was Miss Peppermill and she took me by the hand to my next Therapy treatment . My next therapy treatment was yoga and meditation. None of which I knew anything about. Miss Peppermill gave me a yellow Mat to do the exercises on and then Miss Peppermill laid a Blue mat on the floor for herself. Then Miss Peppermill put some lovely tranquil background Music on, once Miss Peppermill had put the background music on I was shown by her how to do different Yoga positions, how to breathe when stretching in different positions. After the Hour long Yoga session I was tired and Miss-Peppermill told me we could stop for a drink of Water before we moved on to the Meditation. The Meditation Therapy was amazing, I learned all the breathing techniques and being calm and tranquil, breathing is part of relaxing Miss-Peppermill told me. I sat with Miss Peppermill and meditated for a good while, always being reminded by Miss-Peppermill to breathe slowly and relax and let yourself float away. Meditation was very relaxing and then miss-Peppermill clapped her hands and the therapy was over.

Yoga and Meditation Therapy, Great Spa of Aurora

Chinese Fire Cupping, Spa of Aurora

I finished with Miss-Peppermill doing Meditation and the yoga and I was very tired and my next therapy was Chinese Fire Cupping with Miss Chu. I had know idea what this therapy was about.

I waited in the meditation area of the spa for Miss-Chu, Miss Chu arrived and led to the therapy room with Glass round cups on a little table and on the back-wall of the therapy room was seven lit candles, in the middle of the therapy room was a massage table. Miss Chu told me she would leave the room and dis-robe and climb on the massage table and lay on my front with a towel covered over me. I did as requested, then Miss Chu came back in and told me to relax as I was getting excited, Miss Chu started heating the round glass cups with a candle, and then to my surprise put one of the glass round cups on my back. Suddenly I felt a suction on my back. It felt wonderful, after the first glass cup Miss Chu put more cups on me, until I thought my back was being sucked from me. Miss Chu left the cups on my back for 10 minutes and was in a very blissful state. My back felt Great, after 10 minutes Miss-Chu took the cups of my back, one by one, and the glass round cups left a ring marks on my back. These marks where from the suction of the glass cups and Miss Chu told me they would disappear in a couple of hours. I had really enjoyed my Fire Cupping Treatment.

Chinese Fire Cupping, Great Spa of Aurora

Cleaner Fish Treatment, Great Spa of Aurora

y next therapy at the Great Spa of Aurora was with Therapist Kaira and the treatment was a tank full of Water with Glass sides full of Fish. The Therapist Kaira asked me to take of my Robe and use the ladder to climb into the Tank full of Water with the Fish. I did as instructed and got out of my robe and left my swimming shorts on and climbed into the water tank using the ladder.

Once I was in the tank the Therapist Kaira told me to lay in the Water tank and relax, I lay in the tank and then the Fish started nibbling me, they where cleaning my skin, it was a strange experience. The Therapist Kaira told me they where Garra Fish (cleaning fish) and they where cleaning my whole body. I lay in the tank of water with the Garra Fish cleaning my Body for 20 minutes then I got out of the Gara-fish tank and the Therapist Kaira handed me a large towel and wrapped it around me so I wouldn't get cold. Kaira then told me to get a shower and warm up. The Therapist Kaira was right I was getting cold and I quickly got into the Shower to warm myself up. It was a strange experience having Gara-fish cleaning my whole body. At first I was put off by laying in the Water tank with the Gara Fish but after 5 minutes I settled down to be cleaned by the Garra fish and I floated in the Water Tank.

Cleaner Fish Treatment, Great Spa of Aurora

Sleep Study,EEG, Great Spa of Aurora

I finished with the Therpist Kaira at Garra Fish Body Clean and she lead me back to the dining area, Kaira told me to wait in the Spa Dining Area for my next Therapy. I sat in the dining area of the Spa with a cup of tea and waited for the next therapy. As I was drinking my Tea Nurse Thorton and another Lady Doctor with Strawberry Hair walked over to me. The Lady Doctor Greeted me and told me her name was Doctor Millford and the next treatment was going to be a Sleep Study and the Doctor wanted EEG of my Brain Pattern. I followed Dr Millford and Nurse Thorton out of the dining area and along a set of Corridors. Nurse Thorton told me not to be nervous about the Sleep study. We come to the door which had Sleep study on it and Nurse Thorton opened the door and me and Dr Millford walked into the Room. The room was a Bed with lots of Monitors and wires and Medical Equipment, to the left of the room was another room which I could make out as a control room with other Medical monitors and equipment. There was a Chair in the corner of the room with the Bed and medical equipment and monitors. Nurse Thorton told me to sit down in the Chair and Dr Millford would explain what was about to happen in the Sleep Study. I was getting anxious about seeing all the Medical Equipment and Monitors. Nurse Thorton and Dr Millford told me to relax and they explained what was going to happen, they told me I would be wired up to different machines and they would monitor me from the Control Room. First I sat in the Chair and Nurse Thorton started putting round sticky pads on my Forehead and on my face as well, the sticky pads on my Head was EEG (electroencephalogram) to measure and record Brain wave activity. The other sticky pads on my face was EMG (electromyogram) to record muscle activity and EOG by my eyes (electrooculogram) to record eye movement. I was also given a nasal Airflow sensor to record Airflow. The second part I was wired up with sticky pads on my Chest which was a ECG to measure my Heart Rate, two black belts where put around me, one belt was placed around my Chest the other belt was placed around my abdomen to measure my breathing. After being wired up Nurse Thorton and Dr Millford helped me to the Bed in the Sleep Study room. I got in Bed and Nurse Thorton and Dr Millford started connecting the wires to the monitors and making sure they where secured. Once I was wired in and comfortable, Nurse Thorton put a Blood pressure Cuff on my left arm and Oxygen blood peg on my finger to measure how much oxygen I have in blood and Cuff was for my Blood Pressure during the Sleep Study. Nurse Thorton made sure all the wires where connected and working and made sure I was comfortable and Dr Millford fluffed up the pillow for me. I was told to have a lovely Sleep and they would monitor my Sleep Pattern from the Control room. Nurse Thorton caressed my arm and told me to have sweet dreams. Then Doctor Millford and Nurse Thorton went to the Control room. I lay there in the bed in the sleep study room connected to all the medical equipment with wires and tubes all over me. I lay there looking at the pink soothing walls and then I drifted off to sleep, even with all the medical eqiupment wired to me I still went to sleep. I heard someone rustling around the room and I opened my eyes and Nurse Thorton looked down at me and said" Good Morning Sleepy Head, I hope you had a lovely Dream, you have been a sleep for 8 hours". I had a lovely dream about being a Clown fish and swimming amongst the Coral. Nurse Thorton helped me up out of the bed, and while Nurse Thorton was helping me out of the Bed, Dr Millford came into the Sleep Study Room. I sat in the chair in the sleep study room and Nurse started taking the wires and medical equipment of my body and face. Dr Millford told I was Sleep walking during the Sleep Study and I was curled up under the bed at one point. Dr Millford and Nurse Thorton had to put me back to bed after my sleep walking, and they had to re-connect all the wires and the medical equipment. Nurse Thorton showed me where shower room was and I had a Shower and got changed back into my robe and then Nurse Thorton came to collect me for the next treatment at the Great Spa of Aurora.

Sleep Study,EEG, Great Spa of Aurora

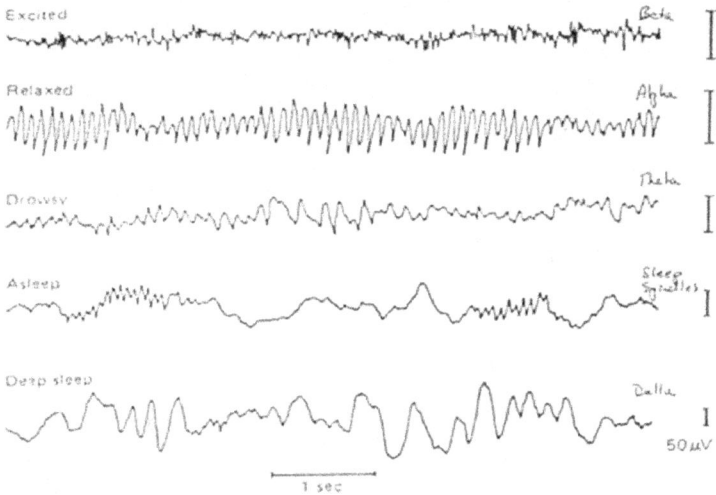

EEG, Brain Wave Activity (electroencephalogram)

Wet Pack Treatment, Great Spa of Aurora

After I had my Shower I got changed into my robe and outside the changing area Nurse Thorton was waiting for me, there was another Nurse with Nurse Thorton and the other Nurse greeted me and told her name was Nurse Louise Halshaw. I noticed next to the Nurses was Gurney with some formidable restraints on it. The Nurses after greeting me undid the restraint straps on the Gurney and asked me to take off my robe and lay on the Gurney. My next treatment they told me required me to be restrained so I didn't hurt myself in anyway. I lay on the Gurney as the Nurses instructed me too and then Nurse Halshaw and Nurse Thorton started restraining me to the Gurney.

First they put a thick wide belt across my chest, then my wrists where restrained with strong padded cuffs, a wide belt was secured across my stomach, and my legs and ankles where secured by restraints. My neck and forehead where restrained by straps and I was very securely strapped to the Gurney by the two Nurses. I wasn't nervous being strapped to the Gurney I actually quite enjoyed it. Once the Nurses knew I was securely held on to the Gurney they started wheeling me down the corridor, all I could see was the pale yellow ceiling as I lay there on the Gurney thinking about what this treatment could possibly be. Nurse Thorton looked down at me while they wheeling me into a room and she was smiling at me and told me to relax. The two Nurses wheeled the Gurney into the room, I could tell we had entered a room I felt the thud of the door open and the ceiling changed a different colour. I felt the two Nurses un-strapping the restraints I had all over my body to keep secured to the Gurney. Then Nurse Thorton told me to lie still I they would shift me over to a table that they had place a Gurney next too. The two Nurses together lifted me onto the table and I immediately felt wet sheets under me. After the two nurses moved me over to the table, they put the Gurney to one side and the two Nurses came back to me and told me I was going to be wrapped up in wet sheets and then I was going to placed in a bath with the water temperature being same temperature as Human Body and a canvas sheet would be placed over the top of the bath and my head would be securely fastened to the canvas sheet. Together the two Nurses wrapped the wet sheets around me and made sure they where tight and the two Nurses where making me into a Mummy and I couldn't move an inch, they where very skilled in this treatment, in know time at all I had become Mummified, it was quite a relaxing experience being mummified and did not mind one bit!. The Two Nurses finished wrapping the wet sheets around me only leaving my face and neck uncovered. Then Nurse Halshaw brought the Gurney back over to the table and the two Nurses shifted me over to the Gurney and secured me to the Gurney using Chest strap and the waist strap. After securing me back on the Gurney in my wet pack, the two Nurses wheeled the Gurney with me on it to the awaiting bath, the bath has metal pipes and taps at the tap end of the bath, and at the other end of the bath was metal pipe that lead away from the bath, I had never seen such a Bath before. The Two Nurses put the Gurney next to the bath and then they lowered the height of the Gurney to the Bath's height I could see canvas straps in the bath to hold me in place in the bath. The two Nurses together shifted me onto the canvas straps that connected to the bath and then the Nurses pushed the Gurney to the end of the Wet Pack Treatment room.

Then the two Nurses went to the other side of the Wet Pack Treatment Room and both Nurses together brought a canvas sheet with a hole at the top of the sheet for my face I presumed.

The two Nurses put the canvas sheet over me and secured the canvas sheet to the bath by using press-studs. The two nurses then made sure my face was secured in the canvas sheet and was out the bath. Once I was secured to the Bath, Nurse Halshaw told me this was a Wet Pack Treatment and I would be in the bath for a good 3 hours. Then Nurse Thorton opened taps on the inlet pipe and water started rushing into the Bath, the water was very soothing and the water was at Body temperature. Then Nurse Halshaw opened the outlet valve of Hydrotherapy Bath.

Wet-Pack Treatment, Spa of Aurora

Chocolate Body Wrap, Great Spa of Aurora

After the Wet Pack treatment by the two nurses I was taken to the Dream room and I had a lovely sleep. After my sleep in the Dream Room I made my way to the dining area of the Spa, I had really enjoyed the Wet Pack Treatment (Hydrotherapy and I was feeling very energized. I waited in the dining area for my next therapy. My next treatment turned out to be a Chocolate Body Wrap and my therapist name was Heather and she told me she loved the idea of me becoming a Giant Chocolate.

Once again I was mummified but this time in Chocolate was put over my body and massaged into the skin from my neck to my feet and I was cocooned with a plastic sheet and layers warm towels. When Heather finished putting the Hot towels on me, she had a Bow with a ribbon attached to the bow and she strapped around my waist and now I had a Big Ribbon on me and I looked like a

Chocolate. While I was mummified in Chocolate the Therapist gave me an Indian Head massage. I was in a very blissful relaxed state being cocooned in Chocolate and having a scalp Massage as well. At the end of treatment Heather gave me a Box of Chocolates and told me to enjoy them in Relaxation area of the Great Spa of which I hadn't been to yet and wondered where it was.

Choclate Body Wrap, Great Spa of Aurora

Relaxation Area, Great Spa of Aurora

After finishing the Chocolate therapy treatment with the Therapist Heather I went looking for the relaxation area of the Great Spa of Aurora. Under my arm I carried the Box of Chocolates that Heather had given me at the end of Chocolate Therapy session. Eventually I found the relaxation area and it was under a Green canopy with a Sun Lounger under the cover of the Green Canopy.

There was also a round table and next to the Table was a Hookah known as a Water pipe and it was all set ready to use. In front of the was a Yellow square slate and to the side of the Sun Lounger was a small statue of a Purple Sperm Whale. On the shelves looked like a Viking Long Boat. I placed the Chocolates on the table. I found out the Hookah is like drinking Herbal Tea, but you breathe in the Vapours. The Hookah was very relaxing and enjoy

154

eating the Chocolates as well. I spent hours in relaxation area of the Spa of Aurora. The Green canopy shaded me from the Sun as I have fair skin and I get sun-burnt easy. I was very relaxed in the relaxation area and had enjoyed all of my treatments at the Great Spa of Aurora. I think the Great Spa of Aurora is amazing, truly relaxing place in the Garden of Aurora.

Relaxation Area, Great Spa of Aurora

Cardio Tilt Test & Cardio Ultrasound, Spa of Aurora

I lay there fully relaxed in the relaxation area of the spa of Aurora for many hours thinking of New Adventures. Nurse Thorton must have found me a sleep in relaxation area as she gave me a shake and told me to wake up. Nurse Thorton told me that they where ready for my next treatment which was to be a Cardio Tilt Test and a Cardio Ultrasound Heart Echogram. I followed Nurse Thorton through the Spa of Aurora to a room with a special bed in it. The Bed had 4 Blue broad straps across it and the room was full of medical Equipment and Monitors, there was also a running machine.

At the side of the room there was a table and an ultrasound machine. The bed looked like it could tilt which I was beginning to realise I would be strapped to this special Bed and have medical equipment strapped to me. Nurse Thorton told me to wait by the ultrasound table, as she undid the straps on the tilt table. Nurse Thrton then told me to remove my Robe and hang it on the back of the door and take my Red Scrub top off and hang it on the Back of the Door with my Pink Robe and to take off my Pink Croc plastic shoes and put the Crocs under the ultrasound table. I did as I was told and put my robe and red scrub top on the Hanger and put the crocs shoes under the Ultrasound table. After I put the crocs plastic shoes under the ultrasound table, Nurse Thorton then asked me to lay down on the Tilt table Bed. I lay on the Tilt table and then Nurse Thorton started putting round sticky pads on my chest. Nurse Thorton told me that this was for a 3 lead ECG and that she would be putting a 12 lead ECG on me as well. Nurse Thorton then connected the wires to all the sticky pads on my upper part of my Body and Arms.

Once Nurse Thorton had connected all the wires to the ECG machines, Nurse Thorton then put a Blood Presure Cuff on my upper left Arm and a smaller Blood pressure cuff on my wrist, on my finger was put a oxygen Blood peg to measure how much oxygen I had in my Blood. Nurse thorton after putting the blood pressure cuff on my arm, then told me she was going to insert intravenous Line into my left Arm in case I needed drugs to speed your Heart back to a normal rate. Then Nurse told me I would feel a "Sharp Scratch" and then she inserted the Intravenous Line into my left wrist.

Nurse Thorton after inserting the I.V Line came to head of the tilt table and looked down at me and explained that I was going to be strapped to the tilt table and then the Bed will move upright Verticle position and she would monitor me to see if I fainted at all, or I become Dizzy.

Then Nurse Thorton after explaining the procedure to me got a white sheet and covered the lower part of my Body so that it was covered over. After Nurse Thorton secured the white sheet for the lower part of my body, then Nurse Thorton secured the Blue velcro straps across me and the Blue velcro straps secured me to the tilt table. Once the straps where put on me, Nurse made sure I was secured to the tilt table and I was wired up to the machines. Nurse Thorton then switched on the ECG Machine and I could hear my Heart beating.

Then once Nurse Thorton was happy, she told me that the tilt table was now going to go upright vertical and if I fainted I would go to the laying position. Nurse Thorton Then Pressed the Button by the side of the Bed and the Tilt Table started moving upwards. I felt quite strange when I was secured to the tilt table upright, I did feel a bit faint but I didn't faint. Nurse Thorton after 20 minutes saw that I hadn't fainted and then sprayed something in my mouth and then I started to feel faint but never fainted. After another ten minutes being upright vertical Nurse Thorton then pressed the Button and the Tilt Table went back to the laying Bed Position. Nurse Thorton then told me she would leave me secured to the tilt table and I would relax and bring my Heart rate back to Normal as I needed to Rest. After 20 Minutes still being strapped to the Tilt table Nurse Thorton undid the straps and she told me sit up.

I sat up on the tilt table and then Nurse Thorton started taking all the medical equipment of me. Only the 3 sticky round pads where left on me for ultrasound test. Once I sat up and Nurse Thorton had removed medical equipment from my upper body, she then gave me a cup of Tea and I would have time to rest before Echo-Cardiogram Ultrasound of my Heart. After 30 minutes resting Nurse Thorton asked me to lie on my side on ultrasound table. I lay on my side on the ultrasound table and Nurse Thorton then connected the wires to the 3 stocky round pads that where still on my chest and she connected the wires to ECG Machine. Then Nurse Thorton put Gel on the Right side of my upper body and then I felt Nurse Thorton put a scanner on my Chest. Nurse Thorton was looking at my Heart through an ultrasound, Nurse Thorton pressed quite hard with the scanner on my Chest and I definitely felt the scanner. After the ultrasound scan of my Heart. Nurse Thorton then cleaned all the Gel off my upper part of my body with tissues and left the 3 sticky round pads in place for my stress test on the treadmill. I ran on the treadmill and I was connected to an ECG machine and blood pressure monitor and ran at different settings that Nurse Thorton had programmed the running Machine. After the stress test I sat down and had a glass of water, Nurse Thorton left the 3 sticky round pads on my chest for the next test, I sat down and Nurse Thorton told me that I had done well with the Cardio test and I completed the Tilt test and ultrasound and stress test, and Nurse Thorton told me she was Happy with the Results.

Cardio Tilt Test, Cardio Ultrasound, Cardio Stress Test, Great Spa of Aurora

02-Max Test, Great Spa of Aurora

I finished the cup of water and I rested for 15 minutes and then Nurse Thorton told me I was going to another medical room to do O2-max test. Nurse Thorton put a plastic Halo ring around my forehead and two metal rods on either side that went down to my nose level and horizontal Bar went under my Nose and joined the metal rods on either side of my face. Then Nurse Thorton put a Nose peg on my Nose and told me to put a mouthpiece in my mouth with tubes connected to it, then Nurse Thorton strapped the mouthpiece around my head so it was secured to my face. Then Nurse Thorton put ECG wires back on my Chest and Blood Pressure Cuff back on my upper arm. Then she told me to get on the Exercise Bike and I would be doing a Max-test t make sure I could do the Extreme Experiences needed for the New Adventures (Chronicles). Nurse Thorton gave me a through test on the O2-max test and I was exhausted at the end O2-max test, my breathing was very hard during the test and Nurse Thorton made sure the Test of the O2-max was tough. After the test I rested, and while I drank a cup of water Nurse came to me with the results of the tests. I had passed the Cardio Tilt Table Test, my Heart was fine on ultrasound, stress test on the treadmill I passed, and the O2-max test I had achieved a high score and I was ready for my New Adventures(The Chronicles).

O2 Max Test, Great Spa of Aurora

Colour Therapy, Great Spa of Aurora

Once Nurse Thorton had finished all the Medical tests, she took me back to the Dining Area of the Great Spa of Aurora. I had a Coffee in the dining area of the Spa and waited for my next Therapy. Suddenly from nowhere Miss-Peppermill was smiling at me and in her hand she had a headdress for me to wear. Miss-Peppermill placed the headdress on my head and asked me to follow her. We arrived in a quite Garden with paint colours in different pots and white paper on the Grass. My next therapy miss-Peppermill told me was Colour Therapy. Together we went through all the colours, Miss-Peppermill told me about different colours and together we painted on the white paper. On one sheet of paper I was asked to write down my New Adventures and I wrote The Chronicles of Nicholas The Red. Miss-Peppermill knew this and told me I was ready to become Nicholas the Red, I enjoyed my Colour Therapy with Miss-Peppermill and we went through lots of Different Colours and I painted on the white paper. Miss-Peppermill told me she had set up a Bed for me outside and I would spend the Night Under the Stars at The Great Spa of Aurora. I sat there with Miss-Peppermill and looked what I wrote, The Chronicles of Nicholas the Red, I thought this was a Beautiful Idea instead of Adventures.

Colour Therapy, Great Spa of Aurora

Night Under the Stars, Great Spa of Aurora

Miss-Peppermill after the Colour Therapy took me too the bed where I spend the night Under the Stars of the Skies of Aurora. By the bed was a Telescope to look at the Night Sky and a Picnic had been laid out for me to eat during the Night. There was a Electric Guitar and amplify to play while I looked at the Night sky of Aurora. I sat over the edge of the wall next to the bed and played the electric guitar and watched the Night Sky of Aurora. The Night Sky of Aurora was Beautiful with lots of stars and planets and bright suns and distance moons. I kept watching the Night Sky and they I saw Felldoran amongst the Stars and planets flying above the Sky of Aurora. I ate some food and then got into the Bed. I lay there for Hours looking at the Night Sky. The Night Sky of Aurora was Wonderous and full of Imagination. I finally drifted off to Sleep

160

under the Night Sky of Aurora. In the morning Miss-Peppermill woke me up and told me I was ready for my New Adventures the Chronicles of Nicholas The Red. I had Breakfast with Miss-Peppermill and Nurse Thorton and I was now ready to become Nicholas The Red and start the Chronicles of Nicholas The Red.

Night Under The Stars of Aurora, Great Spa of Aurora

Preparing to leave The Great Spa of Aurora

After I had breakfast in the Dining area with Nurse Thorton and Miss-Peppermill. Nurse Thorton asked me to follow her to preparation room for my departure from the Spa on the Back of Felldoran the Dragon. I followed Nurse Thorton to a room where there was a square Sarcophagus with Nicholas the Red written on the side, Nurse Thorton told me that was not important right now and she focused my attention to cloak stand with a Tudor Hat on it and a Red Coat, I had enjoyed my time at the Great Spa of Aurora and I was ready to become Nicholas the Red. I started in the Garden of Aurora Study Area where I saw myself in Intensive Care Unit in Hospital and had made my way through the Garden, made it through the Intensive Care Maze to the Great Spa of Spa of

Aurora. I have enjoyed all the treatments at the Great Spa of Aurora. Once I put my new clothes on, I was now ready to climb the stairs with a door at the top of the stairs. I climbed the stairs and Nurse thorton followed me. Nurse Thorton told me that Felldoran The Dragon was waiting for me and I was leaving the Great Spa of Aurora. I was quite excited about riding on the Back of Felldoran the Dragon.

Preparing to Leave the Great Spa of Aurora

Journey with Felldoran, Great Spa of Aurora

I made my way up the stairs and Nurse Thorton followed me and then we came to a clearing where Felldoran the Dragon was waiting for me. I said my goodbye's to Nurse Thorton and then Felldoran told me to climb on Him and get seated in the saddle for the Journey. My Journey was back to my New Adventures, The Chronicles of Nicholas The Red. I climbed on Felldoran the Dragon and got myself comfortable on the Dragon. Then suddenly Felldoran started to Move. Felldoran flapped his wings and Felldoran came to life, the wing span on Felldoran the Dragon was amazing. Then Felldoran pointed his Nose upwards and then Felldoran took flight and I was flying with Felldoran the above the Great Spa of Aurora. Felldoran circled around the Sky of the Great Spa of Aurora and flew past the Great Spa and then Felldoran started to climb above the clouds. My New Adventures awaited, Nicholas the red had been born the life-force and energy was fully restored. In my coat pocket while flying with Felldoran was the time Key of the Garden of Aurora.

Journey With Felldoran The Dragon, Great Spa of Aurora

Nicholas The Red, Above Skies of Garden of Aurora

I flew in the skies of Aurora with Felldoran the Dragon, Felldoran flew high above the skies. I saw in Space the Great Clock in pieces. Felldoran the Dragon told me that he had a Fight with the Great Clock of Aurora. Felldoran told me that I was going to do my Chronicles and Felldoran added I was now Nicholas The Red. I flew with Felldoran for ages flying over the Garden of Aurora. The Blue Sky below me was Beautiful. The Blue and yellow colours of Felldoran The Dragon is dazzling.

Felldoran also told me that as the Clock broke up, The Great Clock had given out a series of numbers, 50,0358 N by 19,1783 E. Felldoran didn't know what this mean't the Great Clock was still powerful. I told Felldoran I still had to find the Heart of the Great Clock. Felldoran the Dragon agreed and I would come back to the

Garden of Aurora to find the Heart of the Great Clock. I took a moment to look at the Sun and the Sun was shining Bright I had enjoyed being being in the Great Spa of Aurora, and the Garden of Aurora.

Nicholas The Red with Felldoran the Dragon, Skies of Garden of Aurora

Chronicles of Nicholas The Red, Garden of Aurora

I closed my eyes and felt the wind on my face above the Skies of Aurora and when I opened my eyes I found myself standing on a white wooden table with a Globe of the Earth in one corner of the white table. To the left of the white table was a series of clock cogs with complex gears turning in time. To the right of the white table was a Heart pumping away. Everything around me was Black and White the Heart was pumping away with no Colour. Suddenly from above me it started raining and the Raindrops where all different colours. It was beautiful standing on the white table watching all the different coloured raindrops. I love colour and I felt a warmth in my heart while watching the coloured raindrops. I didn't understand how i got here as I was flying above the skies of the Garden of Aurora. The coloured raindrops slowly brought colour to the beating

Heart to the right of the white table, and the Heart started beating out all different colours. My colour had returned and I stood there watching all the colours of the Rainbow.

Chronicles of Nicholas The Red, Garden of Aurora

American Diner, Chronicles of Nicholas The Red

I closed my eyes while standing on the white table watching the coloured rain drops and when I opened my eyes I found myself in an American Diner. The waitress was standing over me and told me I had fallen a sleep and asked if I was alright. I asked how long I had been a sleep for, the waitress told me I had been a sleep for only 5 minutes. Then the waitress saw something under the table where I was sitting and she picked it up from under the table, it was a necklace, around disc shape with clock cogs on it. The waitress asked me if I had lost a necklace and told her that I had. The waitress handed me the Necklace. I looked at the necklace and saw it was to do with The Great Clock and I put it around my neck. The American theme Diner was amazing, it had a Juke-box with retro lighting had a small juke-box on the table and had a Pinball-machine in the corner of the American Diner I went over t the

Pinball machine and enjoyed playing on the Pinball machine in the American Themed Diner.

American Diner, Chronicles of Nicholas The Red

The Author Nicholas Robinson

Mayuri (Nicholas Robinson as Geisha) in the Japanese Garden

Nicholas Robinson Feminine CostumesGeisha of Gion, Indian Saree, Marion antoinette Georgian Period Dress

The Helter Skelter Diary Soundtrack
(Music that inspired the Creation of this Diary)

5) Where the Streets have no Name by Band U2
6) Lucy in the Sky with Diamonds by the Beatles
7) Pink" by Aerosmith
8) Smoke on the Water by Deep Purple
9) The Tunnel of Love by Dire Straits
10) anything could happen by Ellie Goulding
11) Wake me up when September Ends by Greenday
12) Rocket Man by Elton John
13) "The Cannonball Run Song" sung by Ray Stevens
14) Loved by the Sun (Film"Legend") Tangerine Dream and Jon Anderson

"The Alchemist Diary"
(Journal of Autistic Adventurer)

The Next Chapter in Nicholas Robinson life with ADHD and Asperger Syndrome sees him going to College and Learning new Skills in 2014.

The Alchemist Diary is a high Octane fusion of ADHD and Asperger Syndrome taken to it's very Limit and Nicholas mixes various Potions together to create Alchemy.

"The Alchemist Diary"
(Journal of Autistic Adventurer)
2015
Written and Drawn by Nicholas Robinson

Nicholas Robinson

Helter Skelter

Nicholas Robinson

www.ingramcontent.com/pod-product-compliance
Lightning Source LLC
Chambersburg PA
CBHW021158010426
R18062100001B/R180621PG41931CBX00028B/49